BRIGHT

ONE FLEW OVER THE CUCKOO'S NEST BY KEN KESEY

Intelligent Education

INFLUENCE PUBLISHERS

Nashville, Tennessee

BRIGHT NOTES: One Flew Over the Cuckoo's Nest

www.BrightNotes.com

ISBN: 978-1-645423-00-3 (Paperback)
ISBN: 978-1-645423-01-0 (eBook)

Published in accordance with the U.S. Copyright Office Orphan Works and Mass Digitization report of the register of copyrights, June 2015.

Originally published by Monarch Press.
John Taylor Gatto, 1972
2019 Edition published by Influence Publishers.

Interior design by Lapiz Digital Services. Cover Design by Thinkpen Designs.

Printed in the United States of America.

Library of Congress Cataloging-in-Publication Data forthcoming.
Names: Intelligent Education
Title: BRIGHT NOTES: One Flew Over the Cuckoo's Nest
Subject: STU004000 STUDY AIDS / Book Notes

CONTENTS

INTRODUCTION TO KEN KESEY

KEN KESEY AND HIS WORK

Ken Elton Kesey was born on September 17, 1935 in La Junta, Colorado. Later, his parents moved to the Eugene - Springfield area of Oregon, where he attended public schools (Kesey was voted the "most likely to succeed" at his high school in Springfield), then the University of Oregon at Eugene. Married to Faye Haxby in his freshman year, Kesey's main undergraduate interests were sports, drama, and writing. His proficiency in wrestling brought him a Fred Lowe Scholarship that paid for a few terms at the University and he also received some football awards. While taking a required course in play - writing (he majored in drama) he became interested in short fiction, and on the basis of a few short stories, he was awarded a Woodrow Wilson Fellowship to Stanford University.

STUDIES UNDER STEGNER

As a graduate student at Stanford, Kesey, studied writing with Wallace Stegner, Frank O'Conner, and Malcolm Cowley. He and his wife took a cottage on Perry Lane, Stanford's bohemian quarter which, according to Tom Wolfe in *The Electric Kool - Aid Acid Test* (a book about Kesey and his "Merry Pranksters") had ... true cultural cachet. Thorstein Veblen had lived there. So had two Nobel Prize winners everybody knew about though the names escaped them. The cottages rented for $60 a month. Getting into Perry Lane was like getting into a club. Everybody who lived there had known somebody else who lived there, or they would never have gotten in, and naturally they got to know each other very closely too, and there was always something of an atmosphere of communal living.

On Perry Lane, Kesey was in close contact with other writers, many of whom have become life - long friends (Larry McMurty, Ken Babbs, Bob Stone, Wendell Berry), and he started to work on a novel called *Zoo*, about San Francisco's North Beach. (An earlier novel about college athletics, *End of Autumn*, written while he was at the University of Oregon, had never been published.)

HIS FIRST "TRIP"

In the spring of 1960, Kesey volunteered for government sponsored drug tests at the VA hospital in Menlo Park. The hospital was paying $20 a session to anyone who would submit to hallucinogenic (or psychometric) drugs, principally LSD and IT-1290. The tests and a cataclysmic effect on Kesey, opening a new world of awareness in which he "could truly see into people for the first time." They were to radically alter his life, and had a direct bearing on his future writing. It is ironic to note that the Federal government, which in 1966 was to sentence Kesey to six months in jail for possession of marijuana, had started him off and paid for his first "trips."

Soon after he began the drug tests, Kesey went to work as an aide in a mental institution in Menlo Park. A Perry Lane friend had suggested he take the job to make some money, and since there wasn't much doing on the night shift, he could work on his novel *Zoo*. But as Kesey became more involved in the life of the institution, he dropped *Zoo* and started to work on *One Flew Over the Cuckoo's Nest*, his first published novel. The book, based on his experiences in the psychiatric ward, was written on the job. Describing his writing habits, Kesey says:

After a few months I settled into a nice midnight - to - eight shift that gave me stretches of five or six hours, five days a week, where I had nothing to do but a little mopping and buffing, check the wards every forty - five minutes with a flashlight, be coherent to the night nurse stopping on her hourly rounds, write my novel, and talk to the sleepless nuts.

"POINT OF VIEW" PROBLEMS

During the early stages of writing *Cuckoo's Nest*, Kesey ran into problems with point of view." He had tried to tell his story through the eyes of McMurphy, the book's **protagonist**, but "something was lacking." In a letter to Ken Babbs, Kesey says:

I am beginning to agree with [Wallace] Stegner that [point of view] is the most important problem in writing. The book I have been doing on the lane is a third person work, but ... I was not free to impress my perceptions and bizarre eye on the god - author who is supposed to be viewing the scene ...

The problem was solved when Kesey, "after choking down eight peyote buds," began telling the story through the eyes of a schizophrenic patient in the Ward, Chief Broom, the book's narrator. Tom Wolfe claims that Chief Broom was Kesey's "great inspiration." By letting the action be seen through the Chief's eyes, Kesey was able to express his own awareness of the essentially schizophrenic nature of existence.

Chief Broom was fictional, purely a product of Kesey's drug stimulated imagination, but many of the other characters in *Cuckoo's Nest* had real - life prototypes among the patients in the ward where Kesey worked. In a second letter to Babbs. Kesey describes some of the originals of *Cuckoo's Nest* characters:

Meternick is tidy, is his bit. No one can touch him. He won't touch on object another has touched. He strips if a towel touches him. He rubbed the hide off the end of his nose after running it up against a patient ...

You know Kramer because he carries his hand tight over his appendix, ready for a quick draw. And has a mean left hook for a feeble octogenarian ...

Pete: grinning ... limping spryly about in his pajamas, answering only one question; - "Why'd you quit driving the truck, Pete?" ...

Kesey put ten months of hard work into *Cuckoo's Nest*, and the book went through many drafts. Much of the original material was written under the influence of LSD and peyote which Kesey took to induce in himself a state of mind similar to that of his narrator, the schizophrenic Indian Chief Broom. Kesey even arranged for a secret shock treatment so he could describe how Chief Broom felt when he came back from electroshock. In *The Acid Test*, Tom Wolfe says: " ... he would write like mad under the drugs. After he came out of it, he could see that a lot of it was junk. But certain passages - like Chief Broom in his schizophrenic fogs - it was true vision... ."

CRITICAL SUCCESS

One Flew Over the Cuckoo's Nest was published by Viking in February, 1962, and was an immediate critical success. *Time* magazine called it "a roar of protest against middlebrow society's Rules and the invisible Rulers who enforce them," and *Life* described the book as "powerful, poetic realism." In the *New York Herald Tribune*, Rose Feld wrote: "for strong writing that holds harsh humor, anger and compassion ... this is a first novel of special worth." Martin Levin in *The New York Times* said: "What Mr. Kesey has done ... is to transform the plight of a ward of inmates in a mental institution into a glittering parable of good and evil." Only one critic, William James Smith in *Commonweal*, had anything negative to say. Expressing his dissatisfaction with Kesey's ending, Smith wrote: "He builds up an atmosphere of real horror and significance and then dispels it ineffectively with some quite misplaced slapstick. The book never gets back firmly on the track and a flurry of activity at the end isn't quite lively enough to disguise the fact that it's getting nowhere." But Smith admitted that "McMurphy and Big Chief Broom ... are character triumphs, and Big Nurse is as near a walking nightmare as you'll come across in this year's literary output."

KESEY'S APPEAL TO YOUTH

During the ten years that followed its publication in 1962, *One Flew Over the Cuckoo's Nest* sold over a million copies. The majority of the readers were under thirty - the age group which most obviously felt the pressure of what Kesey symbolizes in his novel by "the Combine." In 1963 the stage version of *Cuckoo's Nest*, adapted by Dale Wasserman and starring Kirk Douglas, opened on Broadway. Receiving poor reviews it closed after only 82 performances. However, a revised version of the play, produced in 1971 at the off - Broadway Mercer - Hansberry theatre, enjoyed a long run. The success of the play off - Broadway is attributed at least partly to the fact that it was patronized by a younger group than the affluent middle - aged audience which supports Broadway plays. When he attended the Mercer - Hansberry production, Walter Kerr of *The New York Times* observed that the audience - is almost entirely composed of the very young, teeners, early twenties at most ... They weren't far - out kids particularly ... They were the young as the young have always been. But with a difference. The difference was in the play, and in the meanings they took from it ... They have come to attend to an image of what they most fear in their lives, perhaps in the hope of exorcising it by the energy of their applause. What they most fear is just that "conditioning" which is the central action of the play.

In 1962 Kesey moved to the Oregon coast where he began collecting material for his second novel, *Sometimes A Great Notion*. The book was to be about an Oregon logging family, the Stampers, who defy a labor union by continuing their logging operation through a strike. After about four months of research, Kesey went back to Perry Lane where he started writing Notion, then moved to La Honda, California where he spent two years completing it. Shortly before its publication in July of 1964, he wrote to his friend Ken Babbs: "It's a big book ... Perhaps even a great book. If it fails ... and it could fail and still be very close to being a great book - I'll have still learned a hell of a lot about writing from doing it, enough, I hope, to know better than to try anything as cumbersome again." Notion received mixed reviews when it came out. It was praised by *New York Herald Tribune* reviewer, Maurice Dolbier, as a "towering redwood" in the "fictional wilderness." Granville Hicks found it a "fascinating story" that surpassed *Cuckoo's Nest* in many ways, and John

Barkham of *Saturday Review* called it a "huge, turbulent tale" by a novelist of "unusual talent and imagination." On the other hand, Time found it "overwritten" and Orville

Prescott in *The New York Times* blasted it as "the most insufferably pretentious and the most totally tiresome novel I have had to read in many years."

The film version of *Notion*, directed by Paul Newman, was released in 1971. Starring Henry Fonda, Newman and Lee Remick, the picture was highly successful. Rex Reed of the *New York Daily News* wrote: "*Sometimes A Great Notion* ... examines the [Stamper] family's demise, through accidents, deaths and desertions ... By the movie's end, the Stampers have become symbols of a bigger issue: the freedom of man to defend his way of life against outside interference." Archer Winsten of the *Post* said: "What's uppermost is the intransigence of this family which doesn't give an inch, not even to death. What emerges is certainly ... real people ... It is a picture that invites you to take sides ..."

KESEY AND "THE MERRY PRANKSTERS"

After finishing *Notion*, Kesey was in the mood for a vacation. He and a group of friends decided to take a cross - country trip to visit the New York World's Fair (and also to be on hand for publication of *Notion*.) Being in prosperous circumstances then (with income from *Cuckoo's Nest*), Kesey bought an old school bus that had been converted into mobile living quarters. His band of friends, who called themselves the "Merry Pranksters," prepared the bus for the trip, painting it in bright Day - Glo colors, adding an observation deck, and installing some $20,000 worth of movie and sound - recording equipment that Kesey had bought. The group that set out from La Honda in the summer of 1964 included Kesey, his wife, his three young children and about 15 others. The driver was Neal Cassady, the real - life prototype of Dean Moriarty in Jack Kerouac's *On the Road*. They drove across the country, taking films and recording sounds, documenting the communities they passed through and the adventures they encountered. Interviewed for *Publisher's Weekly* when he arrived in New York, Kesey commented on the trip: "The sense of communication in this country has damned near atrophied, but we found as we went along it got easier to make contact with people. If people could just understand it is possible to be different without being a threat - "

"BUSTED"

The trip lasted two months, and Kesey and his friends returned to California with almost 40 hours of film which they planned to edit into a feature - length film. In April of 1965, while they were still in the process of "editing," the Sheriff of San Mateo County arrested Kesey and 13 of the Pranksters for possession of marijuana. The charges against all but Kesey and one other Prankster were dropped, and in December, Kesey was sentenced to six months in jail and three years probation. Meanwhile, Kesey (who was out on bond) and the other Pranksters had initiated a series of Saturday night happenings which they called "The Acid Test." At first these happenings took place in Kesey's home, but as they became more popular, The Acid Test was moved to larger quarters in San Francisco. Finally, Kesey and his Pranksters (along with the then unknown rock group "The Grateful Dead") were scheduled to appear in a three - day rock festival in the huge Longshoremen's Hall on Fishermen's Wharf. However, a few days before the event Kesey was arrested again for possessing marijuana, this time on a San Francisco rooftop in the company of a 19 - year - old Prankster named Carolyn Adams. Once again

Kesey got out on bail, in time to appear in the festival which was a huge success; an estimated 12,000 people attended the festival, largely due to publicity generated by Kesey's second arrest.

In January of 1966, after a third arrest, Kesey fled to Puerto Vallarta, Mexico where he remained for two months - "pranking around," as he puts it - disguised as "mild - mannered reporter Steve Lamb." When he tried to call his wife in California, a well - meaning friend accidentally mentioned the call in the

presence of a newspaper reporter, and the San Francisco headlines screamed "Kesey the Corpse Having a Ball" (to mislead the police, Kesey had left a suicide note in an empty truck on top of a cliff above the sea along the California coast: "Ocean, ocean, I'll beat you in the end. I'll break you this time. I'll go through with my heels at your hungry ribs.") Friends wired Kesey that the police knew of his whereabouts, and after hiding out in Puerto Vallarta jungles for two weeks he made his way to Manzanillo, a tropical beach resort in the state of Colima. Kesey stayed in Manzanillo for the next six months (his family and a number of the Pranksters joined him in the school bus), and it was during this period that he produced 15 lengthy letters (the only writing he had done since *Notion*) to Larry McMurty, the writer whose novel Horseman, Pass By later became the movie Hud. In one of the letters, Kesey ironically appraises his situation:

What was it that had brought a man so high of promise to so low a state in so short a time? Well the answer can be found in just one short word, my friends ...

Dope!

In the fall of 1966, Kesey made his away back to the States, riding a borrowed horse across the border, carrying a guitar, this time disguised as "Singin' Jimmy Anglund." About two weeks after his return he was arrested by the FBI who chanced to spot him on a Bay Area freeway. Kesey was released on bail again, tried on the San Francisco charge, and convicted of a misdemeanor, "knowingly being in a place where marijuana is possessed." Meanwhile, his San Mateo County appeal failed, and in June 1967 he entered jail there to serve almost five months of the original six month sentence. His letters to McMurtry from Mexico were published that year in Ararat. After his release, Kesey and his family moved to a farm in Pleasant Hill, Oregon. During the next year his minor writings appeared in a number of underground journals and rumors were rife in the hip set that he was engaged in a series of transcontinental telepathy experiments with Janet MacAdam, a Prankster from Oyster Bay, Long Island.

He lived briefly in London from March to June of 1969, returning to the United States to a successful opening of a revised version of the *Cuckoo's Nest* play in San Francisco. His probation terminated in July of the following year, during the shooting of the screen version of *Sometimes A Great Notion*. The film was released in 1971.

KESEY'S OTHER WRITINGS

Besides the novels *Cuckoo's Nest* and *Sometimes A Great Notion*, Kesey has written a number of short pieces published by Viking, 1973, as Kesey's *Garage Sale*. In addition, Kesey has edited (with Paul Krassner) *The Last Supplement to The Whole Earth Catalogue*. Kesey is working on a new novel, based on journals he kept while in jail.

ONE FLEW OVER THE CUCKOO'S NEST

....

THE TITLE

The title is drawn from a game, "Tingle Tingle Tangle Toes," played between Bromden and his Grandmother in his boyhood. At the heart of the game is a beast fable which casts in miniature the main tensions of the book:

Tingle, Tingle, Tangle Toes She's a good fisherman Catches hens, puts 'em inna pens Wire blier, limber lock Three geese inna flock One flew east, one flew west One flew over the cuckoo's nest O - U - T spells out Goose swoops down and plucks you out.

From his shock - induced revery, Bromden remembers liking the game and the savior - goose, disliking Mrs. Tingle Tangle Toes. With the revelation of this fable, Kesey has placed a key in the reader's hands with which a major part of the complex, multi - layered thematic substructure may be entered.

A testing of the terms of the fable is required, testing that is, against the characters and incidents of the narrative.

Mrs. Tingle Tangle Toes is, of course, Nurse Ratched, "entangling" victims in her web (recall the spider trope, quite early in Part I) and making them "tingle" in the EST room. The wires and locks of her world are abundantly documented in the Chief's schizophrenic fantasies. On a subtler level is the sex role reversal of wardroom politics: It is Big Nurse who is the fisherman and the things she locks up in pens are hens (i.e., female), precisely what McMurphy has pointed out to Harding and the others - the source of her power lies in her ability to emasculate.

Three geese inna flock are the three main characters whose destinies are intertwined: Big Nurse, RPM, and the Chief. In terms of the artist's mechanics, the line explains why McMurphy has gone through the peculiar ritual of Part I to have himself declared "bull goose looney," a term repeated several times. Additionally it provides insight into the Chief's declaration that he has never been able to hit (shoot) a Canadian goose, although other evidence establishes him as quite a good shot.

This three - goose flock, however, is not together by choice, but by institutional prescription, hence the flock is highly unstable, its members acting upon different motives and toward different goals. The eastering and westering tendencies of the two strongest geese, Big Nurse and RPM, which is to say their pull in different directions, ultimately ruptures the enforced unity of the group. As they go spinning off in opposite directions, the weakest goose, Chief Bromden, freed from their influence, is able to select his own direction, neither East nor West.

One flew East, one flew West ... On the simplest physical level, East and West are polar extremes; tension established by movement in both directions simultaneously creates a force in a third direction, either North or South. Interestingly enough, flight in the book is always conceived of toward the two countries which correspond to North/South from the asylum, Canada and Mexico. Both are spoken well of and the Chief's ultimate destination after his escape is Canada, home of the geese.

East and West in our world are much more than directions, however; they represent the dominant political arenas of the planet and their respective philosophies of Man in relation to the State. The East, at least as popularly conceived, celebrates the group over the individual, encourages confession and betrayal as "therapeutic," values order and regimentation, teaches self - denial and abnegation of ego. There is no doubt that this is the East Kesey means us to consider. The parallel is consciously crafted, from Big Nurse's Oriental placement in the characterization, "big as a Jap statute," to RPM's blunt indictment that the Ward is "a Hell of a lot like a Chinese prison camp." RPM, it will be remembered, holds the DSC for leading an escape from a Communist prison camp in Korea.

On the other hand, "West" as embodied in the McMurphy persona is the antithesis of social engineering with its organization and order. In some respects, Kesey means us to see the pioneer West, a laissez faire, hell-raising, fighting place where each man carves out his own destiny, taking as much as he can get along the way. There is a place for compassion and social obligation in this West but it is every individual's choice just what that place is to be.

Although Kesey's sympathies clearly lie with this way of life in preference to that of the Combine (the code of rugged individualism is drawn even more sharply in *Sometimes A Great Notion*), he is apparently aware of a disturbing dimension in his freewheeling hero. Late in the book, the Chief explains why RPM has been getting the cold shoulder from the other inmates: "You're always ... winning things!" The comment is left undeveloped but the reader should experience little difficulty in seeing the conflict between personal gain and moral leadership.

One flew over the cuckoo's nest ... One (won: the winner) ... cuckoo's nest (colloquial: insane asylum). An apt choice for the title! Who is the one who flies over? It could easily be either RPM or Chief Bromden. Returning to the Chief's childhood rime, we can easily place McMurphy "The Bull Goose" as the hero who selects a penned subject for rescue from among the many supplicants. But with McMurphy's death and the Chief's escape, it is the Indian who flies out of and over the "cuckoo's nest," blown back to full size by McMurphy's blood and strength.

The reader should note that "over," unlike East and West, is not a compass direction, and that in the sense of "above" it expresses a moral relationship as well as a spatial one. Both Bromden and RPM are, indeed, morally superior, at the moment of their flight over the cuckoo's nest, not only to the other inhabitants of the novel, but to their earlier representations.

PHYSICAL AND NARRATIVE STRUCTURE

Cuckoo's Nest is divided into four Parts, further subdivided into 49 scenes. The first part, covering only five days in time, contains almost half the scenes and half the novel's pages. The task of Part I is to introduce the main characters, paint in the sets they will play in front of, indicate their areas of conflict, and plant the seeds of development which will ripen in later sections. Certain key metaphors, like Old Rawler's method of suicide and the fog, are also displayed and a number of preliminary skirmishes are fought between RPM and Big Nurse. These culminate in the crucial scene where Bromden chooses the pain of sanity over the safety of his delusions.

Part II brings a reversal to RPM's fortunes, which leaves the character in no doubt of the seriousness of his situation; the wages of rebellion will be death. Further complicating his decision to contest the field with Big Nurse or maintain a low profile is the revelation that many inmates are self - committed and could "save" themselves by signing out of the hospital. However, when Big Nurse, pressing her advantage, exacts too much tribute as the price of peace, McMurphy commits himself to revolt.

Paralleling McMurphy's narrative is the story of Chief Bromden. The battle for his sanity and manhood is fought through his surrogate, RPM; as McMurphy's fortunes wax, the fog and silence which envelop Bromden recede; as his fortunes wane (or his behavior is less than heroic), the fog and schizophrenic fantasies return.

Part III marks the ascendancy of RPM and his influence over the inmates. He succeeds, in the climactic scene, in bestowing the gift of laughter (and through laughter, power and self - respect) on his disciples, who include the Ward Doctor. In resurrecting these Lazarus from the dead, however, RPM is seriously weakened.

Part IV sees the restoration of Big Nurse's power. His judgment eroded by fatigue, McMurphy plays into her hands by assaulting an attendant. He is sent to the Shock Shop to be reduced to a Vegetable but through an act of will he refuses to be broken. His battle - cry has a radical effect on the Chief, who, by exerting his own will (after RPM's example) wins back his sanity. The recovering inmates, sensing Big Nurse will not rest until RPM is destroyed, urge him to flight; but he refuses until his promise to restore Bibbit to manhood is discharged. During the climactic Bacchanal he is seized, betrayed by Bibbit, and lobotomized. His death, however, is the terminal reversal in the Nurse's fortunes. Her empire dissolves around her as the inmates sign themselves out. McMurphy's sacrifice has made them whole once again. The Chief, restored as McMurphy pledged, smashes the window that restrains him in an act of stupendous, symbolic power, and flies, at last, "over the cuckoo's nest."

MANAGEMENT OF TIME

Kesey goes to great lengths to set his tale in real time, and to allot that time to events in a way the reader can follow. From internal evidence we know the story begins on a Monday in October, 1959 in the election year that saw John Kennedy defeat Richard Nixon. The entire compass of the tale is nine weeks, give or take a day, and all the critical events may be rather precisely dated (from the first World Series game of that year). Dating of this sort, an attempt to tie the novel to the real world, has as its goal a verisimilitude that belongs to the realistic tradition. The theory is that the more fanciful events borrow credibility from the literal ones.

Kesey manages his novelistic time in an interesting way, also. The individual scenes expand and contract (from as little as one - quarter of a page to as much as nineteen pages), creating a definite set of rhythms in the narrative movement.

"POP" ART REFERENCES

A rather large number of pop art references are found in this novel. Several critics, in fact, have pointed to McMurphy as a character out of the Western Movie. Kesey is known to believe that the significant myths of our time are found in comic books, not literature, and on several occasions Bromden refers to the inmates as "cartoons."

Perhaps the most interesting use of pop culture materials in the book is in the employment of the terrible triumvirate of film monsters: Dracula, Frankenstein, and the Wolfman. Upon admission, McMurphy announces he'll be anything that's wanted - even a werewolf - in preference to working in the fields. Later, he tells story of his father who had a ten - inch bolt through his neck - just like the Frankenstein monster. All this is preliminary to the vampire motif that runs throughout the action. McMurphy is figuratively drained of his life by the other inmates who wax fat as he shrivels. In the final Shock Room scene the collective vampire of RPM's disciples is given identity in the form of a "hungry guy," a lunatic, with "a set of long yellow teeth," who importunes the Chief. Bromden has nightmares about his face and asks himself: "That face, just a yellow, starved need ... I wondered how McMurphy slept, plagued by a hundred faces like that, or two hundred, or a thousand."

FLASHBACK

The technique of flashback plays a large role in *Cuckoo's Nest*. It provides biographical data on major and minor characters, and in the case of RPM and especially Chief Bromden it provides a set of cumulative revelations that both foreshadow and interpret the narrative.

EXEMPLARY EXCEPTION

Kesey has a number of unusual social targets which he systematically snipes at throughout the novel, e.g., motherhood, institutional personnel, the hatred and anger of black men toward white, etc.

Because he is aiming at certain behaviors and not at the total individual or institution he needs a way to avoid misinterpretation of his motives. This he achieves by the use of the exemplary exception, that is, by presenting some member of the attacked class who merits praise instead of condemnation. Thus, the sympathetic characterization of the black factory girl and the black hospital attendant, Turkle, stand in antithesis to the circle of black assistants around Big Nurse, who are variously "tarbabies," "niggers," and "Sambos."

FORESHADOWING

Cuckoo's Nest is a very tightly constructed fiction. Consequently it holds no clumsy surprises or **deus ex machina** for the careful reader. All the major actions and events are foreshadowed and flow logically from characterizations and past events. For just a few examples of this consider: RPM's Uncle Hallahan, his Distinguished Service Cross, Mr. Taber, Ellis' crucifixion, and the control - panel scene.

SETTING AND EXPOSITION

As with his management of time, Kesey takes great pains to place his Ward squarely in the realistic mode. The routines of Ward life are painted very clearly and completely. Staff meeting, electroshock, lobotomies, Public Relations Tours, and many other aspects of the institution are managed with such an abundance of detail that they form a very solid and credible stage for the players to walk upon. Just so did Melville operate in *Moby Dick* with the expository whaling sequences.

OFFSTAGE CHARACTER

Cuckoo's Nest makes heavy use of the offstage character, those persons (or possibilities) which, though unseen, affect the actions and understandings of the visible actors. Thus Old Rawler's fate, only remembered by Bromden, yet becomes the literal realization of RPM's warning in the "Pecking Party" sequence.

The Chief can only be understood when his father, mother, and grandmother, the government team, Uncle R & J Wolf, the black factory girl, and his wartime experiences are brought back to life.

And to mention one other among the frequent manifestations of this device, Billy Bibbit's infamous mother, though never seen in the story, has been seen with her chameleon hair "revolving from blond to blue to black and back to blond again every few months."

ALLEGORY

As Barnet, Berman, and Burto put it in their *Study of Literature*, "when St. Augustine noted that we derive pleasure from thinking of holy men as sheep, he was commenting on the pleasure afforded by allegory." Allegory is a form of extended **metaphor** in which objects and persons in a literary work correspond to meanings that lie outside the work. Frequently in allegory, abstractions are given concrete form for the purpose of illustrating a moral, the presumption being that characters and actions will interest us more than the clash of abstractions. *Cuckoo's Nest* contains several allegorical possibilities, chief being The Life of Christ, the political opposition of East and West, and The Destructive Matriarchy.

SYMBOLIC NAMES

Symbolic names have been a favorite tool of writers for many centuries. They are an emblem or banner for the character to display, organizing and interpreting the character's behavior. Randle Patrick McMurphy's symbolic nature lies in the head initials of each of his names (RPM), Nurse Ratched's in its similarity to the word "ratchet," and the author of the important critical judgment on McMurphy ("we must keep one thing in mind: we're not dealing with an ordinary man") is none other than a man named ... Gideon. Gideon was a judge in Biblical Israel (See Judges, chapter 6).

TRAGEDY

Formal tragedy involves disaster, physical, moral, or spiritual. The **catastrophe** results from conflict involving the main character or characters and it ends in the defeat of the hero by his enemies or by impersonal forces.

Tragedy deals with human suffering and human courage; it is an outgrowth of the hero's Resistance. Misfortune and adversity submitted to or complained about do not constitute the requirements of tragedy. The hero must fight, he must comprehend what it is that he is opposing, its invincibility, and what he must ultimately lose as a result of his struggle.

Tragedy involves the idea of hamartia, a tragic flaw in the hero that makes his doom inevitable; it might be pride, an inability to judge situations, or even a virtue that makes his downfall inevitable.

Tragedy recounts an important series of events in the life of a person of significance which culminate in **catastrophe**, the mode of telling being one of high seriousness and dignity. According to Aristotle, the purpose of tragedy is to arouse the emotions of pity and fear and thus to produce in the audience a catharsis of these emotions.

Classical tragedy emphasizes the significance of a choice made by the **protagonist** but dictated by his "flaw," his hamartia.

Cuckoo's Nest participates in the tragic tradition, but it is at once of and yet out of the pattern. It is tragic that McMurphy, a person of significance, is destroyed by resistance to the Combine, but only in a limited way can he be said to have suffered defeat. His death, in fact, signals the end of the Nurse's power over the inmates. Further, his actions, fatal though they are to himself, are absolutely necessary to the restoration of Chief Bromden. In some sense, in fact, he may be said to live on in the person of the Indian.

Yet McMurphy meets many of the tests of the tragic hero. His downfall is brought about by a conscious choice to resist, after having been clearly informed, both directly by the "Lifeguard" and indirectly by several symbolic occurrences, of the fate that lies in store for "disrupters." The fascinating nature of his own tragic flaw is locked within the Tingle Tingle Tangle Toes rime: as the Chief tells us, recounting the childhood game, all the fingers beg to be rescued but the swooping goose plucks only one from the lot.

McMurphy violates the laws of this critical fable. His own escape secure, the Chief (the one finger analog) restored and ready to make his own flight shortly, McMurphy yet lingers to effect the "rescue" of other inmates. But this is to hold in contempt the awesome power of the Combine. His tragic flaw might then variously be seen as too much pride in his own abilities, bad judgment in underrating his opponent, or as the virtue, compassion, in too great a degree.

Whether or not the style of presentation is properly tragic is a moot question. Obviously, for classical audiences Kesey's approach would have been baffling, his selection of a virtual hobo as hero, disgraceful.

But times change and so do interpretations. Our century has been particularly congenial to the idea of the common man as hero (think of Willy Loman in "Death of a Salesman") and the comic mode became, in the '60's, one of the dominant ways to communicate in fiction. Hence, the style alone (which, by the way, has many moments of legitimate gravity and dignity by any standards) cannot absolutely exclude *Cuckoo's Nest* from consideration as tragedy, although it may make for some uneasiness in reconciling it with older exemplars of the form.

DIALOGUE

Dialogue is one of the surest tests of a writer's skills; there are definite standards against which it can be measured:

1. It should be consistent with the character of the speaker.

2. It should contribute to the forward movement of the story rather than delaying that movement or padding the tale.

3. It should give the impression of being real human speech.

4. It should vary in **diction**, phrasing, rhythm, etc., according to the speakers participating.

5. It should present an interplay of ideas and personalities.

Cuckoo's Nest relies heavily on dialogue as a vehicle for its characterizations and ideas. Its rather large cast of talking characters places a severe obligation on the novelist's "ear."

BLACK HUMOR

Although Kesey is hardly a full - fledged black humorist in the manner of Barth or Vonnegut (one critic maintains he cares too much for his people to remain aloof from their pain), the **theme** of laughter as the best specific against the pain and injustice of the universe runs powerfully through the book. There is no laughter on the Ward, as RPM notices immediately, and he knows that "when you lose your laugh you lose your footing."

When, for the first time, the inmates are able to laugh during the fishing trip, a little rain begins to fall - a sure sign that their long winter is over. It is the perspective and wisdom that **black humor** imparts to its possessors that the "cuckoos" (most humorous of birds) must learn from McMurphy: "... you have to laugh at the things that hurt you just to keep yourself in balance." And if we read, as James Miller suggests, *Cuckoo's Nest* as "a paradigm of the predicament of modern man," we must look at our own world as the macrocosm reflected in the asylum - as a vast funny farm. Although the contention is an old one in English letters, it is made with disturbing regularity by contemporary authors and nowhere more explicitly than by Kesey. If we are, indeed, all insane, how singular a phenomenon it is that some of the lunatics should imprison the rest and tell them what to do. Perhaps it is the guards who are the dangerous ones! This is **black comedy** with a vengeance.

Apart from the cosmic **metaphor** the reader finds an abundance of delightful little dark moments, inspired by a sensibility, if not truly black, at least dark grey. When, after the rapture of his first sexual encounter, RPM proposes to his nine - year - old paramour that they commemorate the moment in some way, perhaps by announcing their engagement to their folks, the world - weary little jade gives McMurphy her dress as a souvenir, then replies: "I'll go home in my drawers, announce it that way - they'll get the idea." The reader has only to imagine his own nine - year - old daughter announcing "it" that way to understand the harsh vision that underlies black humor.

THE CHRIST METAPHOR IN "CUCKOO'S NEST"

As critic Richard B. Hauck points out in "The Comic Christ and the Modern Reader" (see Bibliography), the figure of Christ occurs frequently in twentieth - century American novels as a comic figure, introduced consciously by the author in a kind of game between himself and his readers. The game requires the participant to discover the clues which demonstrate a character's divinity and it is often complicated by the moral ambiguity of the selected character.

The selection of comedy as a mode of presentation of an essentially tragic event is, of course, a paradox. Why are the comic and tragic fused? A tentative answer is given by Friedrich Durrenmatt in "Problems of the Theatre":

Tragedy presupposes guilt, despair, moderation, lucidity, vision, a sense of responsibility. In the Punch - and - Judy show of our century, ... there are no more guilty and also, no responsible men. It is always, "We couldn't help it" and "We didn't really want that to happen." And indeed, things happen without anyone in particular being responsible for them... . That is our misfortune, but not our guilt: guilt can exist only as a personal achievement ... Comedy alone is suitable for us ... But the tragic is still possible. We can achieve the tragic out of comedy. We can bring it forth as a frightening moment, as an abyss that opens suddenly; indeed many of Shakespeare's tragedies are already really comedies out of which the tragic arises.

Another possible reason for the use of comedy is that, in a cynical age such as ours, it serves to disarm the reader, to attract our sympathies. A serious treatment of the Christ **metaphor** as tragic hero, doomed son, or social scapegoat would be antithetical to the American temper, might run the risk of "turning us off." If the power inherent in the savior myth is not to be dissipated, the author must seduce us into accepting his own interpretation through the device of sympathetic characterization.

Kesey solves this problem with his Christ figure, R.P. Murphy, by casting him to appeal to the American taste for broadly played, irreverent humor. McMurphy is a drifter, a conman, a gambler, a practical joker: an ironically incongruous combination of traits for a savior.

All the necessary clues for an identification are baldly, even sarcastically presented, as if Kesey were taking a gratuitous swipe at his own presumption in reworking the myth (and indirectly giving the horse laugh to all self - consciously symbol - ridden prose). For instance, on RPM's first night in the asylum he appears ready for bed in coal - black satin undershorts covered with red - eyed white whales (a clear **allusion** to Melville's *Moby Dick*) and tells Chief Bromden: "From a co - ed at Oregon State, Chief, a Literary major... . She gave them to me because she said I was a symbol." When he is being prepared for electroshock therapy, he asks the technician: "Do I get a crown of thorns?" He remonstrates with the inmates for "... coming to me like I was some kind of savior."

He has the physical presence of a God. Sometimes when he walks his boot heels "cracked lightning out of the tiles" and when he moves in to punish his antagonist Big Nurse, in Chief Bromden's words: "... here he comes and he's big as a house!" At the hospital staff conference the doctor announces: "No one can say this is an ordinary man we're dealing with." In a deliberate echo of Christ as the Big Fisherman or "fisher of men," McMurphy takes twelve of his followers on a fishing expedition: "McMurphy led the twelve ... toward the ocean." (The ocean, the "father of waters," is variously a symbolic statement of wholeness, oneness, strength, regeneration, Nature, and the Infinite Mystery; and water itself is one of the most commonly employed symbols in literature.) Even Big Nurse is aware of the alter ego, literally the "other I" in McMurphy. She charges him with two deaths, saying "I hope you're finally satisfied. Playing with human lives - gambling with human lives - as if you thought yourself to be a God!"

Identification of McMurphy as a Christ surrogate is only the first step in prying the Christ **metaphor** loose from its literary context. If the writer is a craftsman, as Kesey certainly is, we should be able to trace, through the device of parallelism, at least three other major developments of the Christ story:

1. The character will preach (can we find a Gospel according to RPM?)

2. His practice will find imitators (what of disciples?)

3. He will be crucified and his crucifixion will have a conversion effect (we need to locate an analog for crucifixion, and to find some significant character development that occurs as a result of his death)

While many other parallels are utilized by writers in employing Christ as a literary figure, these three central motifs recur over and over. We should expect to find them in *One Flew Over the Cuckoo's Nest*.

GOSPEL ACCORDING TO MCMURPHY

Gospels, in the generic sense, are the glad tidings of the Kingdom of God (see Matthew, chapter 4). They are revelations, guides to human action, interpretations of the Christian message. We should expect McMurphy, as a gospeler, to produce collectible teachings, and indeed he does, but naturally their promulgation must be indirect since the novel and the sermon are antagonistic forms. We learn the McMurphy canon from his own statements, describing himself or interpreting some event, and from conclusions drawn by the other characters who are most affected by his actions, notably Chief Bromden, but also Harding, Scanlon and others. The major teachings of RPM, reinforced and made evident by Kesey's frequent restatements, are ten in number:

1. You're safe as long as you can laugh. Open up and laugh; when you lose your laugh you lose your footing, your grasp on life.

2. True wisdom is largely innate, inherent in your biological nature. The influence of others is a weakening force. Be yourself and what you want to be.

3. Persist in the face of opposition. Don't give up the ship - and don't let the "givens" of your life, physical or situational, limit your choices.

4. Life is a gamble for stakes. Play not to win, but to try the impossible, the prize is in the effort. Remember: honest self - interest equals sanity.

5. Intense and diversified experiences makes a full life, not careers and routines. And sexual experience is a central business of living, a fundamental good.

6. Be aware and analytical. Look the game over before you draw a hand.

7. Be adaptable, not rigid.

8. Freedom goes to the wary. Stay free of bonds, even self - imposed ones. Travel lightfooted and fast; a moving target is hard to hit.

9. A man's destiny is always in his own hands.

10. Bravado and courage are sources of power, and physical contests are necessary to preserve one's integrity.

THE DISCIPLES

The other inmates very quickly begin to function as McMurphy's disciples: they serve him, imitate him, and repeat his teachings. Twelve of the men go fishing in the ocean on an expedition planned and led by him. And without exhausting the parallels, we can point to Billy Bibbit as McMurphy's Judas - for it is Billy, who McMurphy has delayed his planned escape for, who confesses to Miss Ratched, implicating McMurphy to save himself. An interesting project for a literary detective with some time on his hands might be to draw as many analogies as the text will support between the original Biblical dozen and RPM's crew.

CRUCIFIXION, CONVERSION, RESURRECTION

Kesey makes no attempt to be subtle here. He has previously let us know through the agency of Harding that men are crucified on the shock treatment table. Now, when RPM is led to the cross he asks the technician, "Do I get a crown of thorns?" After his death, the voluntarily committed inmates, no longer the "rabbits" of Harding's diatribe, discharge themselves from the asylum, effectively destroying the organization Big Nurse had constructed with their compliance. They are McMurphy's men now, still with their problems, but able to laugh and see them in perspective. The conversion is complete.

With Broom's escape, RPM's promise to make the Chief whole again comes true. As once the Chief's hand was "pumped up" to life size with the energy from McMurphy's hand, now, with the sacrifice of his entire life the Chief's body becomes gigantic once again. His returning strength enables him to lift the enormous control - panel and send it crashing through the asylum's restraints.

He is once again Tee Ah Millatoona, the Pine - That - Stands - Tallest - on - the - Mountain! But he is at the same time more than that - he is the Bull Goose flying over the cuckoo's nest, as McMurphy was before him. Strong, free, unbound by the ties of **convention**, he holds within him the resurrected spirit of McMurphy, which in a masterful involution of the title parable, he has swooped down and plucked from the world of insanity!

The reader who examines Kesey's **parody** of Christ will be struck by the power implicit in this form of comic presentation. There is a laugh, yes, but there is also wisdom and sadness in the replay of an ancient story on a modern stage. The elements of **satire** in the construction are never turned toward the idea of Redemption and a Redeemer, but only toward the academic "symbol - industry" that often pursues its metaphorical quarry in a humorless, disproportionate quest that misses the point of literature.

It has been argued that only a comic presentation of the Christ myth will cause the cynical modern reader to temporarily suspend his disbelief and listen. While this is certainly moot, it does appear that contemporary writers of stature believe it to be true, and the practice is not all uncommon in recent fiction.

ONE FLEW OVER THE
CUCKOO'S NEST

PART I

. . . .

MORNING ON THE WARD

Morning

A time of freshness, innocence, new beginnings; here twisted into a time of hate, fear, and weakness. By opening the book with the very opening of the new day, Kesey will be able to show us from start to finish the literal, hour - by - hour horror and emptiness of institutional life. As in the first visible act of the attendants' day we witness the brutalization of the first patient to rise. ("Here's the Chief. The soo - pah Chief, fellas. Ol' Chief Broom. Here you go, Chief Broom ..."), so the attendants are then brutalized in their turn as the first visible act of the Head Nurse's day.

Kesey sets the stage quickly. In short order we are given the time, the day (Monday: another beginning) and some of the Ward's morning routines. Ample clues indicate this is no normal ward: the attendants' disrespect manifested openly, the patronizing tone of the Nurse, but most of all, the decidedly peculiar actions and perceptions of the narrator.

Appearance And Reality

One of the tasks that Kesey sets himself in *Cuckoo's Nest* is to challenge our notions of what is real, to have us plumb the depths of "what seems to be" in order to discover "what is." The narrator's grotesque exaggerations would seem to mark him as insane and therefore an unsympathetic character - yet the wealth of vivid detail in his observation, the objective reporting of dialogue and actions that controvert his fantasies and thus allow the reader a "normal" perspective, the pathos of his childhood memories, the fear he has of his keepers and their cruelty toward him, all these things combine to make him an agreeable and interesting companion and guide for the reader, one who, curiously, seems quite trust - worthy (lacking the guile to deliberately lie), intelligent, and sympathetic. The reader quickly sees that something is going on here, that something is being kept from him, but that only serves to heighten interest in the game, especially considering the fact that the game appears to pose no great effort to follow. (For contrast, consider Faulkner's Benjy and the rigorous discipline necessary to play his -idiot's game.)

The narrator discloses immediately that he has maintained the guise of deaf mute for years, the reason why "hate and death and other hospital secrets" have not been concealed from him as they have from other patients - the pretended infirmities have made him of so little consequence to institutional personnel that he is virtually invisible. In a sense this partly frees him from the imprisonment of the traditional first - person narrator, as he will be privy to all the secrets of the cuckoo's nest.

If the half - breed Indian is something more than the pitiable "Chief Broom," then the Nurse herself is not only the buxom, neatly tailored middle - aged woman in the starched white uniform and woven wicker bag. When no one is looking, "she really lets herself go...." Regardless of the fact the reader knows immediately this is not literal truth, the image is so well drawn, so suggestive, that it broadcasts a kind of poetic truth and we are convinced that something real and menacing lies behind the fanciful description.

Power And Control

On one level, *Cuckoo's Nest* is a political novel, dealing with the nature of power and control, who has it, how it flows, its effects on the people it is directed against and on the people who wield it. The black boys revel in their power over Bromden. One swats the backs of his legs with a broom - handle to hurry him past, then gloats. The Nurse's power, metaphorized in a fantastic mechanical - etymological trope, is directed first toward the black boys whom she cows into submission, next toward the patients whom she "crashes ... outta her way with that wicker bag." Since power is at least the sum total of the strengths of those dominated, we get a rough index of Big Nurse's force: one black boy is superior to one Indian Chief; Big Nurse is superior to three black boys and a ward of patients.

Still another, more sophisticated kind of power manifests itself in this initial scene (which foreshadows later crucial developments); it is the power that comes from self - control, from "cooling it." The Chief gives us a highly instructive parable drawn from his boyhood memories: in sum it is the lesson that a bird is safe from its hunters as long as it can remain still (maintain self - control), but if the constant and terrifying pressure of the search makes the bird break from cover, then it is lost.

Metaphors And Motifs

Three key **metaphors** whose repetition gives them the status of motifs occur in this scene. The first is the essential mechanical nature of Big Nurse and the black attendants. Although they are more than simple machines, being able to assume monstrous aspects, they are less than human.

The second is the fog that snows down around the Chief, so that he is unable to see reality. Sometimes the Chief can hide in the fog, but like the bluetick hound he is scared and lost because he cannot see.

Third is the Combine, the mysterious organization that has rigged the Ward with devices for spying and control.

Time Perspective

The action starts in media res and it is only at scene's end we realize the narrator is looking back on the events described. Although the present tense is maintained throughout the narrative, giving Kesey the advantages that unfolding action offer a writer, we will remain aware it is a history we are witnessing. This device serves, as does the Chief's deaf - mute disguise, to partly free the narrator from some of the traditional first - person restrictions, especially as they concern such a speaker operating in the present. We may now allow some observations from Bromden that would seem too lucid for his schizophrenic persona.

Artistic Truth

Stepping directly out of the narrative, Kesey, through Bromden, makes a dramatic appeal to the reader arguing the significance of what is about to take place. He is concerned that his story be read as more than story - that it be seen as Truth. Implicit in his plea is the contention that reality can exist on other planes than the simplistic relation of objective occurrence.

THE NEW ADMISSION

Ward Routine

The narrator continues to discuss, with great precision, the routines of the Ward. A chronology of daily events is beginning to emerge and we are amazed that this apparent lunatic, debased to the extent that he wets his bed, observes events so closely. We are even more amazed to learn that he is capable of sarcasm and critical judgment - his condemnation of the Public Relations Man's blindness to, or unconcern for, actual conditions is verified by the glimpses we have already had of petty cruelties visited on the patients by the staff.

Our guide is capable of integrating his perceptions and interpreting them as well - note how neatly he dispatches the band of school teachers with the ironic observation that they are "bunched together for safety" (if their fear is so manifest what must they teach the young of insanity?) And in one quick stroke he shows us the sterility and boredom of Ward life: every time the door opens (as it does "a thousand times a day"), "all the heads come up like there's strings on them."

Wealth of concrete detail and matter - of - fact information about the Ward is a key element in Kesey's design. It is important to his purpose that we not dismiss out - of - hand the fantastic parts of his tale before we have grasped the true nature of the Combine, the conspiracy to regiment our lives. If the Chief is just a cuckoo, then his ramblings will be inconsequential, but if he can be shown, objectively, to be something more, then his paranoid visions may partake of the credence that parts of our culture have historically extended to the visions and prophetic power of the insane. A cynical age such as our own will not automatically accept this power; therefore, Kesey must prepare the way by demonstrating the Chief is saner and more intelligent than his situation should warrant.

Characterization

Kesey is extremely skillful at dynamic characterization, more frequently an attribute of dramatists than of novelists. Dynamic characterization results from "showing" character traits through action rather than announcing them. Instead of calling the Public Relations Man a sanctimonious hypocrite, Kesey selects a scene from his life. By allowing us to watch it, we come to the same conclusion ourselves - with the important difference that instead of being lectured to (an unpleasant and boring business), we have participated in the creation of the character. No longer spectators, we are involved.

The Admission As Myth Figure

Paralleling the literal narrative throughout the novel will be an allegorical strain: McMurphy as the Redeemer (see section: The Christ Metaphor). Kesey wastes no time opening the ground for this construction: Bromden, who can only hear the new admission, McMurphy (making him invisible, as a supernatural figure should be), nevertheless states baldly: "Still, even though I can't see him, I know he's no ordinary Admission." Later, the reader will realize that this is Bromden's heightened sensitivity and prophetic power at work, but for the present, sound observations are available to defend the judgment. In the first place the admission doesn't slink around in fear as strangers to the cuckoo's nest are apt to do; in the second, he refuses to subject himself to the black boys; in fact, he establishes himself as master by addressing them in a good humored, derogatory fashion. Then there is the matter of his voice, loud and booming, and the queer position (vis - a - vis the attendants) it appears to emanate from: "He sounds like he's way above them ..."

Kesey is not content simply to establish RPM as a Christ figure. He proposes, in the same scene, to establish him, additionally, as that favorite popular culture myth figure - The Western Hero! The **parody** is not accidental. Kesey is aware that convincing his cynical, highly educated and symbol - blase audience that RPM is Christ and that perhaps, just perhaps, the Combine really does exist, will be no easy task. He will lull our suspicions with laughter and the image of a hip author who knows what the score really is. Later, when our defenses are down, when we have identified with the Chief and McMurphy, when we have recoiled with recognition at the horrors of the institution, then, and only then, it will be time for ... The Greatest Story Ever Told.

Motivation

It is important to justify McMurphy's act in coming to the asylum, lest he be just a more colorful Crazy than the others. Motivation, too, is one of the surest measures of great fictional art, just as unconvincing motivation is a sign of the pedestrian hack. Behavior must spring from the nature and circumstances of the character, the more inevitable and impelling, the better. It is all right to say that McMurphy, as Christ, has come to the cuckoo's nest to redeem the inhabitants, but this will hardly do as a fit reason for a brawling, hell-raising drifter. What will do, however, is the opportunistic explanation: The asylum food is better, the work is easier, the "pigeons" riper, than on a prison work farm; therefore he has "arranged" a transfer for himself. There is a third possibility, too. The "court," after all, sentenced him to this "establishment"; perhaps he is, in conventional terms, insane! Kesey displays here his consummate skill at ambiguity. All three of these threads are woven into his tapestry and will surface again and again.

Theme And Motif

Four motifs emerge in this scene. They will recur over and over, in slightly different forms each time, but always signaling a thematic constellation associated with the McMurphy character.

1. Laughter - Notice that laughter has been absent from this insane asylum. Bromden says, "It's the first laugh I've heard in years."

2. Lusty sexuality - Best expressed in RPM's own words: "Who ever heard of a man getting too much poozle?"

3. Gambling - "I'm a gambling fool." Think of gambling as an opposing trait to caution, as taking a chance on the possible, not "playing it safe."

4. Resistance - He resists the black boys, but remember, too, he has been sent to the asylum for constant fighting.

THE DAY ROOM

A House Divided

The opening part of this scene, while ostensibly continuing an objective description of the workings of the asylum, is describing on another level a world split asunder and kept that way by its overlords. The Day Room is the gathering place of the patients who, we learn, are divided by staff judgments of whether they can be cured or not into two groups, Acutes and Chronics. Division by diagnosis is translated into physical division of the two groups into opposite sides of the room, enforced by the subtle coercion of the black boys who want it that way because it is "more orderly," which we may take to mean easier to supervise. The Chronics are further divided (and thus even easier to classify and manage) into Walkers, Wheelers, and Vegetables. Note the clear allegorical message: to the Establishment, the highest value is cooperation with the authorities.

The administration has devised a way to separate the more active Acutes and prevent any incipient cohesion among them - it has encouraged a flourishing spy system in which every man listens to the words and actions of his companions in order to glean tidbits of "therapeutic interest" - for which the spy is then rewarded. It is the old strategy of "Divide and Conquer" which figures so prominently in Machiavelli's *The Prince*. The embarrassing information is then discussed publicly in "Group Meeting," an exercise in which Big Nurse can detect and destroy any signs of burgeoning individualism in its earliest stages.

Into this twilight world comes the new admission. Revolutions Per Minute, blowing fuses in the Combine's Control Panel with the sound of his laughter and his prescient assessment: "You boys don't look so crazy to me."

He will assume the obligation of reuniting the people of this world, putting the jigsaw back together, but this can only be done if they recognize his leadership. His actions are quick and decisive: "Take me to your leader and we'll get it straightened out who's gonna be boss around here."

This last quotation works quite well as a statement of the central, literal conflict of *Cuckoo's Nest*. It will take the entire book, though, to "get it straightened out" for, as we will shortly learn, the leader is not Harding, but that awesome agent of the Combine ... Big Nurse Ratched.

In the meantime, McMurphy engineers a symbolic unification of the Ward, bringing the men together by his own example as he passes from Acutes to Chronics, shaking every man's hand with his own tough, battlescarred lunchhook. The patients are baffled, because his motivation, his "real world" motivation, that is, is hidden. And, or course, on the multi - level allegorical plane of the novel he does have a gambler's reason for his behavior, for he is to play poker for these men's souls in a cosmic poker game with the Big Nurse. To win they must ultimately trust him more than they fear her. Unifying them will be the equivalent of holding a straight flush - the Combine senses this and that is why the men are kept alone, discouraged from fraternizing, mistrustful of each other.

And Big Nurse senses the danger from her new admission. In the climactic moment of this scene she makes an appearance to warn McMurphy that everybody is subject to the rules. At which point McMurphy restates the resistance motif and foreshadows his main course of action from that moment forward.

Foreshadowing

Cuckoo's Nest is a deliberately constructed work of art, at all times under its creator's control. The reader who is concerned with extracting the maximum understanding from the somewhat rare experience of dealing with a literary architect (who understands how to allot his resources for maximum effect) should understand that in a book like this Nothing Happens By Accident! Every brick laid must eventually accumulate to form a structure. This process, known as **foreshadowing**, adds greatly to the suspense a practiced reader looks for and enjoys in great fiction. In this, the third scene of the book, Kesey offers us three harbingers of things to come, all of which will have important effects on the resolution of *Cuckoo's Nest*:

1. Ellis His brain has been short - circuited by electroshock therapy, one of the staff "mistakes." Now he stands as a mock - Christ, crucified to the wall, his catatonic position an echo of the cruciform shape of the shock table. He is a symbol of the power the staff wields as well as a warning to McMurphy that playing Christ is a dangerous game in the cuckoo's nest.

2. Ruckly Ruckly is Ellis raised one power. He, too, is a warning to McMurphy for at one time he was McMurphy - like - a "holy nuisance ... kicking the black boys, biting the student nurses" ... so they took him away to be fixed. Ruckly has been lobotomized, the ultimate weapon in the Combine armory. Resistance is a dangerous game, too, in the cuckoo's nest.

3. Billy Bibbit "If I was d - d - deaf I would kill myself."
    Here is a much more indirect sort of **foreshadowing** -
    a rhetorical "if ... then" conditional threat from an
    apparently meaningless character. But this warning,
    ignored as are the others, is to cost McMurphy a great
    deal of effort and concern, and, in the end, his life.

Each of these characters foreshadows important events to
follow in the narrative. The perceptive reader, understanding
this process, possesses still another ticket to participate in the
construction of the novel, equal with dynamic characterization
in its power to induce audience involvement.

Supernatural Power

Scene three adds another evidence of supernatural power to
McMurphy's stock, a power we shall call the ability to see into
people. As we might expect from Kesey, the master of ambiguity,
the power may simply be another manifestation of the Chief's
paranoia, since it is remarked by the Chief and is about the Chief,
but it is nonetheless impressive.

In the course of circulating through the list of Chronics,
shaking their hands, RPM eventually comes upon the Chief who
discerns instantly that McMurphy is "onto" him: "he wasn't
fooled for an instant by my deaf - and - dumb act." A startling
insight since we know that Bromden is the senior patient,
has been on the Ward for years, and has fooled the Nurse, the
attendants, the other patients, and the "Combine" all that time.
By implied contrast we realize how potent his "vision" is.

As the scene closes we learn of yet another power of
McMurphy's: through the laying on of his powerful hand he can

pump energy and strength into another person "like he was transmitting his own blood." This reverse - vampirism will figure large in the resolution of *Cuckoo's Nest*; taken alone it is still a compelling image and indicates another of Kesey's strengths as a writer - the ability to create powerful and exciting images which grow organically out of the plot development.

The Combine

The steady accumulation of mechanistic **imagery**, from the first page of *Cuckoo's Nest* until its conclusion, is connected to an organizing fantasy of Chief Bromden's which he refers to as the "Combine." The Combine may be seen as a paranoid delusion, the Indian's own particular bete noire which he uses to rationalize his own disturbed behavior. It may be, but as the reader soon discovers, this turns out to be an unsatisfying and unsatisfactory usage. Bromden is too sympathetic a character, too easy to identify with, for the reader not to give some credence to the Combine as a poet's creation, a way to explain and give meaning to the inhumanity of the institution (and, by extrapolation, the world). A third possibility will not be quelled: that is, of course, that the Chief has perceived something real, perhaps not all of it and perhaps imperfectly, but real nevertheless.

We shall return to the Combine later; suffice it to say for now that the Combine is an impressive artistic conception: it gives the support to the construction of Bromden's insanity; it provides a slowly unfolding mystery and with it, welcome suspense; it provides a frame for what would otherwise be many disconnected bits of information; it is a vehicle for social satire, relieving Kesey of the burden of finding a way to say "isn't this awful?; it has overtones and undertones which reverberate into all corners of society including the reader's own - all of these things are important labors performed by this marvelous child of Kesey's imagination.

But by far the most important single contribution of this idea is to the dramatic scaffolding of *Cuckoo's Nest*. For his **protagonist** to gain heroic stature he must have an antagonist worthy of him. The Nurse and her armory of weapons will be a most formidable foe for McMurphy, but as an agent of the all - powerful, earth - girdling, brain - destroying association of technocrats she will be both formidable and diabolical. As Kesey realizes, the only proper foe for a God - figure is ... The Devil!

THE NURSE'S STATION

Motivation

We are shown McMurphy's motives for action from the Nurse's point of view in a brief scene designed to lend credibility to her position. She has seen "manipulators" before - sometimes acting for power or respect, comfort, monetary gain ... or simply disruption for the sake of disruption - the clients of the institution are insane. She recalls a tough customer she once dealt with, and though we are given no explanation, we note she seems pleased with the memory. Thus Kesey prepares us for a crucial scene to come.

Characterization

Even in this brief scene we can see Kesey's method of dynamic characterization working: the needle - filling procedure, the response to Miss Flinn, the pleasant memory of "Mis - tur Tay - bur" are bits of action - painting from which conclusions about the character can be drawn. This style is also known as the dramatic method because it is the traditional way to establish character in the drama. Kesey was active in theater during his college days.

ONE FLEW OVER THE CUCKOO'S NEST

. . . .

BIG NURSE AND HER WORLD

Chief Bromden's Perspective

After scattering clues to the nature of the asylum world throughout the opening, Kesey decides to halt the narrative and tie these clues together into a systematic perspective that gives us a history of the Ward - at least as Chief Bromden believes it to be. We see that the Ward itself is a factory for the Combine, dedicated to repairing mistakes made in school, churches and other adjustment mechanisms on the Outside. On the Ward, Inside, twisted and different "things" are "fixed up good as new, better than new sometimes."

Whatever her nominal position in the institution, Big Nurse is in charge. She has accumulated her ideal staff, i.e., those in harmony with her design: her attendants are caricatures of men (notice they are always referred to as "boys"); their one overdeveloped characteristic is the ability to hate. Originally they preferred direct means to express their rage at deviants, but Big Nurse has trained them in subtler methods. The Ward doctor is tolerated because he is ineffectual, a "little man."

The goal of Big Nurse (and the Combine) is a world of precision, efficiency, and tidiness. Kesey compares it to a pocket watch with a glass back - "a place where the schedule is unbreakable." In such a world, Man exists to serve the Machine, not the reverse. And the Nurse, heavily cloaked with Kesey's mechanical metaphors, is certainly just that - a machine, sitting in the center of a web of wires "like a watchful robot," tending her network "with mechanical insect skill." In such a world there is neither grief nor happiness, nobody dies, they only burn out and are recycled; actually, it is a rather safe place, everything is planned - there are neither risks nor surprises. The biggest difficulty in Nurse Ratched's job lies in adjusting new admissions to the pattern; the biggest fear, an admission who has escaped Combine - conditioning on the outside and might upset the applecart.

Characterization

If an author concentrates on a dominant personality trait to the exclusion of all others, a type of characterization called caricature results. When caricatures occur accidentally in fiction, it is a sign of the author's lack of control over his creation; on the other hand it is quite possible deliberately to create caricatures that are striking and useful to the author's purpose. This is clearly what Kesey has done in this scene. The Nurse is a caricature living through her malevolent passion for order; the black boys are caricatures energized by hate; the doctor is a stock figure from **burlesque**, the mousy intellectual, and all the patients are caricatures whose traits are punched onto an IBM card and are available on command.

In this scene it is Kesey's purpose to arrest the credibility of his own puppets, temporarily, by forcing the reader to acknowledge the clumsy artifice a caricature really is. In fact, the point is so important to a proper understanding of *Cuckoo's Nest* that on five separate occasions in this scene Kesey directly states that these characters are cartoons! At a juncture like this in a serious work of fiction, with the author flashing lights and waving flags at his reader, as it were, it is incumbent upon the student to ask himself - Why? In this case, why the apparent self - parody?

The answer is that Kesey has selected a form of **irony** to convey his horror and disgust at the **dehumanization** the institution effects under the guise of ... Humanity! In literary circles the caricature is acknowledged as inhuman, unbelievable. Kesey agrees, yet still makes his inmates and attendants all caricatures - and makes sure the reader knows about it. He is saying, in effect, "These characters are unbelievable, unreal, like cartoons - but they really are that way! The institution has stripped the inmates and its own personnel of their human characteristics - only caricatures are left to characterize!"

At the same time, Kesey has provided us with a unique way to measure RPM's progress as a Redeemer. We need not speculate or interpret events; to the extent that his actions cause the caricatures to lift off the page, to break their patterns and round out a bit, we will be able to visibly measure his effect on the cuckoo's nest.

Social Satire

Kesey can't resist taking a swipe at the "well - adjusted" man's life, the man whose life was planned, who never made any waves, and who "adjusted" his wife and kids to the same wavelength. His reward when he "runs down" is a picture in the local paper, a letter from the High School Principal, and maybe, just maybe, a discount from the embalmer. Seen from this vantage the "good life" seems good ... for nothing.

Another Warning

The Chief's memory of Maxwell Taber is the third direct signal that Big Nurse's bite is worse than her bark. Kesey means the reader to bear this in mind during the raucous comedy scenes to come in which RPM appears to emerge victorious.

The Microcosm

It is obvious that the Ward is intended as a miniature world that Kesey feels will represent the larger world or some part of it Bromden provides two analogs to the Ward in this scene: the touching cotton - mill memory in which the Chief recalls a still "living" human being struggling to escape her assigned web where all about her were "adjusted," and a fleeting memory of the tribe, after its land was gone, working on the dam, "faces hypnotized by routine."

Motivation

Why do the Combine, the Big Nurse, and other "adjusted" types behave the way they do? Although Kesey suggests some tentative answers throughout the book, he never undertakes a comprehensive **exposition** of motives. Rather, he seems to say, this passion for order, this anti - life force we may call it, is a Given in the universe, like black holes or entropy. It must be answered with Resistance: boldness, swagger, risk - taking, lovemaking - all the things that are its antithesis. There is some connection made between the Combine and the world of women, though the connection is implied rather than explicit; this will be discussed later.

THE GROUP MEETING

Sexuality Motif

There is some reason to believe that male sexuality is one of the prime targets of the Combine, representing, as it does, the tendency toward disorder and animality as opposed to predictable machine order. Big Nurse, her unusual breast development notwithstanding, is asexual as is Dr. Spivey; the black boys' specialty is unnatural acts with helpless patients; and the inmates themselves have been neutered by humiliation. McMurphy, however, is exuberantly sexual. His story of the fifteen - year - old hustler at Group Meeting is a link in a long chain of sexual "events" that arise from McMurphy. His pornographic playing cards, his constant innuendo, his swagger, his songs, his undershorts, his tales of conquest, his friends on the Outside - all are a counterweight to the sterility of the Ward. He announces his "sickness" proudly; significantly it is a part of his record the Nurse has "overlooked." There is response to his open sexuality from his sexless companions, but it is guarded subdued amusement, tight and dry. The only evidence available that these have ever been loving men is the tormented **parody** of passion,

Rackley, whose injunction about the wife echoes through the meeting.

Point Of View

The point of view wavers for a moment in this scene as Kesey feels the need to examine McMurphy's thought. At the close we are getting information from an omniscient narrator. Hardly noticeable to the general reader, such an inconsistency is reckoned a flaw by the trained eye as it suggests a temporary loss of control.

Conflict

The first open skirmishing between Big Nurse and RPM occurs in this scene. As McMurphy has received warnings of Big Nurse's potency, so now he delivers a warning to her in the form of the story about his Uncle Hallahan, perhaps apocryphal.

THE THERAPEUTIC COMMUNITY

The Theory

In a superb **parody** of a New *York Review of Books* - style intellectual, obsessed by his own cleverness and blind to the world as it exists beyond the comfortable reach of his own voice, Kesey constructs the rationalization for all the training and "rehabilitation" institutions of modern man and puts the speech in Dr. Spivey's timid mouth.

Part of the **satire** here is directed against language itself, a protest against the hollowness of words. The doctor's prescription seems wise, measured, sane, eminently fair, but what is the reality these words describe? We have seen what happened to Mr. Taber when he exercised a "little gripe." The constant "squealing" and involuntary group discussions have eroded the cohesion of the group and obviated the possibility of friendships. As for democracy being the principle of the Ward, that will remain true precisely as long as nobody tries to act out a democratic scenario - like a High School Student Council.

What then are we to conclude? That Dr. Spivey is a monster? Or a liar? No, what Kesey is driving at here and elsewhere in *Cuckoo's Nest* is that words and meaningless routines insulate people from life itself, blind them to what is happening around them, and deaden the moral faculties. The great criminals of our century have been bureaucrats with high ideas and common men just "doing their jobs." Heller saw this clearly in *Catch-22* and, in fact, it has become a customary **theme** in the modern novel, particularly a staple in black comedy.

Dramatic Verification

It is characteristic of Kesey's style that theory, stated or implied, must be dramatically illustrated. Immediately after the **exposition** of The Theory of the Therapeutic Community, Bromden recalls a Group Meeting where, to please Big Nurse, and escape the excruciating tension of honest silence, the inmates frantically confessed to the vilest crimes their imaginations could conceive.

Symbolic Contrast I

Chief Bromden escapes participation in these character - destroying exercises through his self - imposed silence - as the American Indian as a group has been silent in the councils of the nation.

Symbolic Contrast II

In the Group Meeting, the behavior of one of the Chronics, Pete Bancini, is riddled with symbolic elements which Kesey uses to reflect light on the Acutes and to outline a course of action for dealing with the institution, a counter - prescription to the Therapeutic Community. Bancini interrupts the meeting with the symbolic shout "I'm tired!" delivered in an angry voice that no one has ever heard from him before. The utter honesty of the statement, with its implication (actually delivered somewhat later) that "... it's a lotta baloney," shames the Acutes whose sycophantic confessions are shown for what they are - whimperings of half - men under the lash of the Master. When the black boys try to remove Bancini, he produces a symbolic reaction to the violation, responding with violence, a course which instantly earns him the respect of the aggressors and a hands - off policy, too. Next, in a scrap of **exposition** on the "life of Bancini" we learn that, although a literal imbecile, he has held a responsible job all his life through "main force and ... gutpower," an illustration of one of McMurphy's motifs, "trying," and perhaps the central moral statement of the book. Bancini delivers a scathing reproach to the Acutes, drawing the analogy between his experience and theirs. Bancini shines like a moral beacon, for this brief moment, in the Waste Land.

Theme And Internal Conflict

With the Bancini incident in hand we begin to be aware that the external conflicts of *Cuckoo's Nest* will be joined by a vital internal conflict. We can no longer see the tale simply as RPM vs. Big Nurse or even as two ways of life in violent opposition - for now the possibility has been sounded that the Chief and the inmates are not being victimized by external forces, but are victimizing themselves and creating, or at least tolerating, their own Hells. One of the deeply - rooted **conventions** of serious literature, by the way, has been to put critical or prophetic utterances into the mouths of madmen or fools, as Kesey has done here.

THE PECKING PARTY

Extended Metaphor

In the longest scene in the book, McMurphy instructs Harding (and through Harding the other inmates) in the emasculating design of Big Nurse. Likening the group meeting to a "pecking party" (a form of animal behavior in which chickens rip one of their wounded fellows to shreds) and the Nurse to the chicken who inflicts the first wound to start the slaughter, RPM brushes aside Harding's ineffectual opposition and states directly that the target of her attentions is the masculine principle, symbolized by the testicles.

Harding's half - hearted defense, showing Big Nurse delivering charity baskets to the poor, is ironic in the extreme since the reader clearly sees that her effect is to sow guilt and discord, reflecting, as she does, on the lack of cleanliness in the donee's house and on the inability of the husband to properly clothe his wife. It is evident that Kesey extends this satirical sketch to include all charity that operates in this fashion, destroying self - respect. Soon, however, Harding drops the mask of intellectual fairness, acknowledging the truth of McMurphy's insights. And when Harding is won over, the rest of the Acutes begin to follow. The first tentative steps toward communion, real group identity, have been taken.

Style

Animal **metaphors** delineating human traits are as old as literature itself. McMurphy's "chicken" **metaphor** gives way to Harding's "wolf and rabbits," but the principle in both is the same: it is often possible to see more clearly by not looking directly at the object of your attentions, but at a reflection of it. Kesey's skill with **simile** is evident in this scene, as elsewhere. Consider this one describing Harding's tortured laugh: "A sound comes out of his mouth like a nail being crowbarred out of a plank of green pine; Eee - eee - eee." (Note, too, the use of onomatopoeia and noun - as - verb.) It would be a mistake for the student to regard metaphorical usages like this as an ornament of style. Rather, they should be seen, when properly employed, as a fundamental and irreplaceable technique of communication. For many things **metaphor** is the most accurate resource language can offer.

Conflict Alteration

When McMurphy draws the terms of the wager in which he bets that he can demonstrate the vincibility of Big Nurse, an important stage in conflict development has been reached.

Until this point, the opposition of the two figures arises from unplanned encounters between strong, antithetical personalities. Now nature gives way to conscious design. McMurphy will deliberately set out to bring Big Nurse down. This development should be seen as a critical stage in the metamorphosis of McMurphy the Man into McMurphy the Hero. For the hero must choose his course of action, his destiny - not arrive there by accident.

Theme And Symbol

"We are victims of a matriarchy here," says Harding. This symbolic utterance is meant to be taken seriously, in the particular scene in the microcosm of *Cuckoo's Nest*, and in the secular world of the reader. Over thirty female characters are seen, heard, and talked about in the novel and much of the male characters' difficulties result from the women in their lives. Bromden's mother has emasculated his father, stealing his self - respect, even denying his name; Ruckley's experience with marriage can be summed up in the only communique he cares enough to deliver to his fellow man, "Ffffffuck da wife!"; Billy Bibbit's "fiance" greets his proposal with laughter, his mother imposes a lifelong childishness on her "boy"; Harding's wife mocks his delicate sexuality, turning her husband into a "diseased rabbit"; Mrs. Tingle - Tangle Toes and Big Nurse like to lock things into pens; and on and on. The target, of course, is not the specific women cited, but the values of the matriarchy, which Kesey apparently sees in historical terms as worship of authority, order, neatness, guilt, repressed sexuality, hypocrisy, backbiting, caution, planning, couth, vengeance, fear of difference, and corrosive envy of maleness and its attributes. Although not necessary, it is possible to read Combine and

Matriarchy as equivalencies in Kesey's scheme and to make a strong case for the equation.

SANTA CLAUS

After the tension of the previous scenes, Kesey indulges a bit of comic relief, the admission, adjustment, and dismissal of Santa Claus. Comic interludes are consciously introduced by an author to offer relief from emotional intensity and, by contrast, to heighten the seriousness of the story. The gravedigger scene in Hamlet and the drunken porter scene in Macbeth are famous examples.

EVENING: THE FIRST DAY

Time - Control Metaphor

The Chief's paranoia endows Big Nurse with superhuman powers, among them the ability to control time, speeding and slowing it at her whim. Some days the inmates are made to rush through the entire schedule twenty times an hour, until they are exhausted - this is done during the times the inmates want to hold, to make last, as when they have a visitor or when there is a show. But generally the clock that controls Ward time is slowed down by the Nurse or stopped so that time doesn't move at all, the hands of the clock are frozen at two minutes to three. The time - control **metaphor** serves three important functions: it grounds and verifies (as do all his fantasies) the Chief's sickness, his internal mental state; it cloaks the Nurse with devastating symbolic power, continuing the process of building her into a worthy antagonist for a hero; and it enables the reader to participate in the sensual reality of asylum - time and feel its essential meaninglessness and absurdity.

Symbolism

A useful instance of the way symbolism functions in literature, operating on multiple levels and delivering vital information, is found in the card game As part of the dealer's patter, he delivers each card with a verbal flourish. Note Harding's: "too bad, another lady and the Professor flunks his exams ..." The card is first of all a card and occasions a colorful bit of dialogue; next it is a "lady," as such setting up correspondences with the matriarchy **theme** and with Harding's difficulties with his wife; finally, and significantly, it is a queen, colloquial parlance for a homosexual. The evidence of this, laid down in previous scenes, is confirmed by the symbolic card; we are now prepared to view Harding as a man unable to come to terms with his repressed homosexual nature.

LIGHTS OUT

McMurphy's last act on this, his first day on the Ward, is to "see through" the Chief's pretended dumb show, a clarity of vision the Nurse could not manage in fifteen years of control. The discovery was foreshadowed in the day - room scene and now comes to pass because of RPM's talent as a close observer of events.

Motifs

Sexuality and laughter, two key motifs associated with McMurphy and his "Therapeutic Community," figure in this scene, His laugh has "banged around the day - room all evening" but it has failed to bring a sympathetic response from the inmates (when this comes it will be a mark of progress toward Redemption). As the men are preparing for bed, McMurphy makes an abortive movement toward the night nurse's breasts, to her terror and Catholic consternation (the church is satirized here as antisexual medicine, the cross being "popped" into the nurses's mouth like a pill!).

Symbolism

A number of prominent symbols occur in this scene, including one intended to be a **satire** on symbolism itself - McMurphy's "white whale" shorts, an **allusion** to *Moby Dick*, itself a prodigiously symbolic work. The shorts have been given to him by a girl, who tells him he is a symbol! Here Kesey takes a kindly swipe at the symbol - making establishment of which he is a part. The tattoos are Life and Death, the Fighting Leatherneck representing the vigorous maleness of McMurphy and the "devilish" strain that popular myth has always seen in masculine men; the poker hand, aces and eights, being the famous "dead man's hand" of Western lore. Last, and most important, are McMurphy's own hands. We have just seen that he carries "the dead man's hand" on his body, but his own hands are the legendary "healing hands," the hands of life that faith healers use in revival meetings. The symbolic, magical nature of McMurphy's hands recurs frequently in *Cuckoo's Nest*, the hands becoming a motif of the protagonist. They have been used to pump life into Bromden's arm, to de - crucify Ellis, to bring play into the Ward by dealing cards, to get rid of the drugs that cloud Bromden's mind, and to offer sexual encounter to the night nurse - all this by the end of his first day on the Ward. Note too that stylistically, the hands are well conceived.

THE NIGHTMARE VISION

The night of McMurphy's admission, Chief Bromden has a surreal nightmare, a vision compounded partly out of the events that drove him insane (although we don't realize this until later), partly out of his systematized delusion, the Combine, and partly from the events of life on the Ward seen through a distorting glass. The vision is brought about by missing his sleeping pill and by the death of the Chronic Blastic while the rest of the Ward sleeps. It is a vision of "relentless brute power" glimpsed by the Chief as the floor of the Ward sinks into some subterranean chamber filled with machines and blast furnaces and workers with "dreamy doll faces" (a link to Big Nurse) who race through the vast inhuman factory spinning dials, pushing buttons, throwing switches. It is the vision of a technological Hell. The Chief locates it in the bowels of a giant, hydroelectric dam, "where people get cut up by robot workers." This is an **allusion** to his tribe, cut up, too, by "robot" workers.

Theme And Motif

The scene is essentially restatement of earlier thematic material in surreal, stream - of - consciousness form. Life is reduced to mechanism, evil is shown as intrinsically banal, possible through the complicity (or perhaps the casual disregard) of the common man. Blastic's death is of no more consequence than the scrapping of a broken clock. The emasculation motif comes back in a bizarre dramatic costume as the Public Relations Man, revealed as a corset - wearing grotesque, minces through the dream and adds Blastic's organ to his collection.

The Fog

The fog that clouds the Chief's vision has an ambivalent nature. It isolates and confuses him, true, but insofar as it prevents him from seeing the world the way it really is, it makes his life tolerable, defending him from things he does not want to see, to "face." Fog serves as a barometer of Bromden's sanity; as he progresses toward "full size" the fog recedes, as he retreats back into fantasy the fog advances. In addition the movement of the fog measures the relative ascendancy of Big Nurse or McMurphy, his victories dispelling it, hers summoning it to return.

Appearance And Reality

The reader might well ask why Mr. Turkle, the black aide introduced in this scene, is, unlike the other black attendants, not a "boy" (he is called a man) nor a target for epithets like "coon," "tarbaby" and "nigger."

The answer lies in his approach to his job, other people, and himself. Implicit in Kesey's value - system is a belief that might be worded this way: "Give disrespect where disrespect is due - and in whatever terms suit best." Thus the black attendants fall prey to racial slurs, except Mr. Turkle, whose dealings with the world prove him fully human.

THE TOOTHPASTE INCIDENT

Structure

Almost one - third of the book has been devoted to McMurphy's first day on the Ward. Now, at the beginning of his second day, the battle lines have been drawn between the contending forces, one is almost tempted to say between McMurphy in the white trunks and Big Nurse in the black trunks. The boxing analogy is apt. The first rounds of a fight between well - matched opponents are used for sparring, skirmishing, feeling an opponent out. The first "rounds" of *Cuckoo's Nest* are used in similar fashion. But the time is now at hand for more serious slugging. McMurphy, the contender, will have to prove himself early against the heavy artillery of Big Nurse if he hopes to win the crowd. From this point until the end, Part I is divided into two "Movements," both fueled by the bet made by McMurphy in scene 8, after the Group Meeting. The first of these movements will comprise five scenes and be constituted of a stirring series of small - scale McMurphy triumphs over Big Nurse and the Institution. The second movement will comprise seven scenes of substantial ambiguity. Based on the Chief's apprehension and retreat into fantasy, it will appear that McMurphy's forces are in confusion, threatened with rout. The strength and resources of patience at Big Nurse's command show their rock - ribbed outline now as they did not when McMurphy was pilling up victories. Finally, just when it appears that Big Nurse has closed for the knockout punch, McMurphy pulls a dazzling reversal, snatching victory from defeat and closing Part I. The flow of these two movements is quite distinct. Armed with the knowledge of their existence, the student should attempt to experience them as rhythms, tidal movements that form part of the living structure of the novel.

Social Satire

The institution, and its lackeys who give homage to its meaningless proscriptions, take a good punch in this scene. When McMurphy is barred from the toothpaste because it is not time for the toothpaste, he is the victim of a kind of foolishness we all have suffered and which seems endemic to bureaucracies - the sanctity of routine over human variation. It may take all kinds of people to make a world, as the saying goes, but the bureaucratic world is made for one kind of person, in this case a person who brushes his teeth at 6:45 A.M. To the astonishment of the institutional personnel, McMurphy neither complies nor rebels, he merely demonstrates the highest form of intelligence, flexibility or adaptability, finds a substitute, unrestricted cleanser, and brushes his teeth at his own chosen time. Self - reliance, he says in effect, is the antidote to institutional stupidity.

Singing

The second morning stands in stark contrast with the first. Instead of Chief Bromden's dark fantasy, we have McMurphy's joyful song of male - domination and roguishness. It startles the Acutes and makes them doubt the power of the black boys - why haven't they hushed him up. Song often occurs in literature as a symbol of life - affirmation.

BIG NURSE LOSES HER COOL

Anger

The only emotion Big Nurse allows herself is anger, but anger represents a danger to her position as it potentially signals a loss of control. Therefore she is practiced at keeping her temper under wraps - patience and pressure, guilt - inducing and innuendo replacing it as her first line of response to people who need comeuppance. To get the best of the Nurse, according to the terms of the Bet, we can then expect McMurphy to try to stimulate her to public rage, where any loss of control, however temporary, can be translated into loss of prestige.

Sexuality Motif

Lusty sexuality, in the shape of unashamed nudity, creates the basis for McMurphy's next victory. His first move, baffling the nurse's henchman, is quickly followed by a series of actions aimed directly at Ratched's composure. Learning of the toothpaste incident, which offends her sense of order, Big Nurse rumbles after a singing McMurphy, only to be confronted by him, nearly nude, a blow at her carefully nurtured asexuality. A **burlesque** scene follows in which, under the guise of being compliant, McMurphy threatens to remove the towel completely, unsettling Ratched still further. Ultimately, McMurphy does remove the towel, draping it over the woman's shoulder (to indicate disrespect) and revealing not nakedness but the outrageous black shorts with "those big white whales leaping round."

Characterization

Big Nurse's power is caught in two splendid images. The first is a **metaphysical** conceit (a complex, startling, highly intellectualized analogy) in which she appears as an enormous truck, smashing along the highway "trailing that wicker bag behind in her exhaust like a semi behind a Jimmy Diesel ... her smile's going out before her like a radiator grill. I can smell the hot oil and magneto spark when she goes past, and every step hits the floor she blows up a size bigger, blowing and puffing, roll down anything in her path!" The second image, also a conceit, illustrates her immense self - control. According to the implicit terms of the novel, at all costs Big Nurse must conceal her humanity (to this point housed in her breasts and her anger) in order to retain her power. Unwilling to allow the patients to see her face "white and warped with fury" she masters her anger in a startling passage: "Gradually the lips gather together again ... run together, like the red hot wire had got hot enough to melt, shimmer a second, then click solid as the molten metal example, in Billy.

Motivation

On the literal level, Kesey needs some way to explain Big Nurse's power over the inmates. He accomplishes his purpose by establishing her as a mother surrogate, the patients as children, and the controlling mechanism her ability to instill and nourish strong guilt feelings in the men, for example, un Billy.

Social Satire

Kesey means us to generalize from Big Nurse's system of control and emasculation through guilt to mothers in general. Billy Bibbit's mother, the most obvious parallel, is described as Miss Ratched's friend. Later, we learn that Bromden's mother has used the same technique to destroy her husband and son.

MAN SMELL

Symbolism

Smell, the least "civilized" of the senses, is hardly discussed at all in polite society; yet we understand that something valuable has been lost in suppressing this information - channel, hence we accord respect and credibility to those "primitives" who still retain the power to "smell things the way they really are."

The smell continuum may be divided into natural and un - natural smells, the former invoking strong and pleasant associations, the latter varying, depending upon what they have been paired with in the memory. Institutional smells seldom give rise to good associations, but perhaps none call up such unpleasant mental pictures as those of a hospital, whose smells bring back associations of isolation, immobility, sickness, pain, and death. Surrounded by these hospital odors, Bromden (a "primitive" retaining his olfactory power) smells "man smell" for the first time in fifteen years. Thus does Kesey discover another device to tell the reader that the sickness on the Ward is that its inhabitants have been de - humanized.

ONE FLEW OVER THE
CUCKOO'S NEST

. . . .

BREAKFAST

Structure And Point - Of - View

One of the difficulties in the dramatic method Kesey employs is that subtle plot turns may be missed in the excitement of action. To avoid this, he endows the Chief at times with an almost omniscient understanding of developments, which he relays to the reader. In the breakfast scene Bromden tells us that Big Nurse's early defeats have only put her on guard; in fact, they have made her stronger!

Characterization

McMurphy's early successes make him ebullient. Although he still can't bring the men to open laughter, he does cause them to grin and snigger, a measure of returning strength in RPM's value system. He again reveals himself as adaptable to any conditions - in the sense that he has the power to make his surroundings accommodate some design of his own. He is delighted with his comfortable bed and the lavish breakfast, in stark contrast to the glumness of his tablemates; when he learns breakfast must continue until an arbitrary time, regardless of when the meal is actually finished, he invents a game that diverts him, amuses his companions, and controverts the solemnity of the institutional moment. This must be seen as another victory in his string, this time a victory over himself as well as the Combine.

THE SECOND GROUP MEETING

Structure

This is by far the most complicated scene to this point, consisting of a series of six contests (one implied) between Big Nurse and McMurphy. The dramatic peak is reached when McMurphy, seemingly beaten in the matter of the carnival (doubly depressing since the tide of opinion appeared certain to carry the day for him), pulls a rabbit out of his hat, dealing a smashing blow to Big Nurse in the form of the tub - room coup, hammering it home with the assistance of Dr. Spivey (the figurative rabbit) who stands, however shakily, against her opposition - his own strength marking another victory for McMurphy as well. In an insulting anticlimax, McMurphy caps his accomplishment by seizing the floor at Group Meeting, literally silencing Miss Ratched.

Reversal

Expectation that defeat will crack Big Nurse is not realized, however, her superb self - control manifesting itself beautifully while the tide runs against her. This unexpected development throws Bromden into despair. As the scene closes, thick swirls of fog roll into the Ward. Bromden welcomes the safety and concealment as it closes around him.

Motivation

Bromden has expected, or at least hoped, that defeat would crack the Nurse. But her stoic relentlessness is more than he can bear; in his weakened condition he has no stamina to sustain a fighting spirit; therefore, he retreats into the fog.

Irony

McMurphy announces his tub - room victory through Spivey, the very spokesman Big Nurse had used to squash the carnival plan. That the vehicle for her winning should become, moments later, the vehicle for her losing is an example of **irony**, neatly handled.

Theme And Motif

Doctor Spivey's show of strength occurs after he emerges from McMurphy's intake - interview looking "like he's actually been laughing"; his collapse on the carnival idea in the face of Big Nurse's opposition occurs after she has infected him with guilt that he has made such a decision without consulting the staff. This clash of antagonistic motifs is brilliantly worked out throughout the book.

Dramatic Necessity

Big Nurse has taken McMurphy's best shot and survived; the Chief is disconsolate; what can possibly happen to shake up this woman in the few days remaining on the Bet? Given Kesey's love for comic myth, we can almost hear him think to himself ... this looks like a job for.... Supermannnnn!!!

Symbolism

The sound the radio produces is an "infernal noise" because, by preventing conversation, it isolates the men. It is another device, like her log-book - spying - system, to keep the men alone and helpless. A well known military policy dating back to classical times provides a useful caption for this strategy: divide and conquer.

Appearance And Reality

The Nurse appears reasonable in her explanation why the music cannot be turned down, but since a solution to accommodate both Chronics and Acutes is available, her refusal to even consider it seriously reveals the reality behind appearances.

THE MONOPOLY GAME

Again, a brief scene played for comic relief. This time, however, there are a number of undertones. In this imaginary universe of the game every man is God, slinging houses, hotels and stacks of brightly colored money around in a heady fashion. Every man makes his own decisions and wins or loses accordingly. In addition, the game and the idea of playing together is a necessary preliminary to group identification and laughter, both parts of RPM's design. Laughter has already been amply explained as RPM's sovereign specific, but as the next scene will show, McMurphy is standing alone against An Organization. He needs help. One way to get it is to weld the disorganized Acutes, natural enemies of Big Nurse, into a friendly band.

Symbolic Irony

McMurphy's monopoly "Chance" card elects him Chairman Of The Board, but the reward for this honor is to … pay every player! He comments prophetically, "Boogered and double boogered!"

THE CONTROL PANEL

Symbolism

Following the relief of the monopoly game, Kesey gives us an extremely complex scene, shot through with intricately interdependent symbols. The way out of the asylum, he instructs the Acutes, is literally to throw out the control panel, on a physical level smashing the reinforced windows, on a symbolic spiritual level becoming independent of rules, orders, and other people's urgencies. Significantly, he himself is unable to do this! (We will learn much later just who is controlling McMurphy.) He pays a heavy price for his effort, however, losing back all the money he has won, and tearing the palms of his hands so that they bleed. "It'd take a giant to lift it off the ground," says Chief Bromden, **foreshadowing** the novel's resolution wherein

McMurphy's power as Redeemer is proved when a giant does just that.

Literary Technique

A fascinating, inadvertent glimpse of literary craft in the building stage shows up in McMurphy's comment: "... there's at least twelve of you guys I know of myself got a little personal interest who wins these games." The **allusion** is to Christ's disciples, and it may have been Kesey's original intention to portray twelve Acutes as disciple - analogs. However we know that later to fill out a complement of twelve on the fishing trip, McMurphy needs to take the Doctor and Candy, the prostitute. These inconsistencies are almost always reconciled in the rewrite stage, but occasionally a few remain to remind us how far removed from simple storytelling a serious work of art really is.

Theme and Motif

The emasculation motif (Harding's: "... I am afraid she'll cut it off if I raise it") signals the presence of the matriarchy. Since we know that one of the principal effects of the matriarchy is to keep men as children, it is doubly significant that Cheswick characterizes the Ward as "Ol' Mother Ratched's Therapeutic Nursery." This is followed by McMurphy's contemptuous putdown, "... your mamma probably wouldn't let you cross the street." A secondary effect of the matriarchy is to Feminize Men (remember the Public Relations Man), so it is no surprise when another McMurphy putdown comes out as "... you bunch of old ladies."

Motivation

As the scene opens we find the inmates in the throes of recidivism, sunk back into the isolation of their individual pockets of fog. McMurphy's attempts to stimulate them to act together in their own interests (changing the TV schedule by vote so they can see the World Series) fail - ostensibly for good reasons - but actually because they have long ago lost faith in their power to affect their own destiny. Believing they are powerless, they see no reason to choose to do anything. Bibbit's statement of futility is really not a statement at all, but a question put to McMurphy (and every Redeemer) by those he would lead: "... what's the use ...?"

No further plot development is possible in *Cuckoo's Nest* until an answer to this motivational question is given. And the answer to Bibbit's question simply is - because the exercise will do you good. The dramatic illustration of this answer comes with McMurphy's attempt to do the impossible and lift the control panel. It is the effort, the "try" that does a man good. Action is its own reward, the key to sanity. His ringing challenge at the scene's close reinforces the lesson: "... I tried ..." This is the answer to Billy Bibbit's question and it will provide the motivating engine for the balance of the novel.

INTO THE PICTURE

Structure and Motivation

This short scene and the two following, each a specimen of the Chief's paranoid fantasy, mark a crisis in the development of the Bromden character. Confused and unsettled by McMurphy's assault on the control panel in the previous scene and the implied threat RPM is to the established realities of his life for the past fifteen years, he reaches a crisis, a fulcrum point which can tip him, seesaw - like, back into his delusions or forward to renewed growth.

Symbolism

The picture is an unreal representation of the world and yet it is more real, more sensuous than all the hospital world with its visiting "authorities." The shivering Doctor implies that on some level the institutional personnel are aware of this, too. The genesis for this fantasy is the picture's echo of Bromden's lost reality.

THE FOG

Symbolism

A restatement of the safety - in - invisibility idea, this time paired with two images (crawling on hands and knees and sticking gum to furniture), makes Kesey's meaning clear. To be invisible, safe because you are of no consequence, is to accept the powerlessness of childhood. But unlike the "matriarchy's" saccharine memory of that time, the intelligent adult knows it to be a nightmare filled with schedules, orders, punishments, guilt, and a denial of insistent, awakening sexuality. Chief Bromden has reached an important choice point (and choice is the hallmark of growing up); he must face what it means to stand out of the fog, with all its dangers, or sink back into an endless childhood.

Literary Technique

A turnaround has taken place in the Bromden character, but Kesey must be careful to bring it along slowly, always motivating the development and allowing for a naturalistic "backing and filling" process to simulate the real - world processes of personality change. A character who moves this way belongs to a typology known as the Developing Character, a pole part from the unchanging character (represented here by Nurse Ratched) which we call Static Character. Unmotivated or unconvincing development, common in popular fiction, is called False Development.

THE SUICIDE

An interlude of sardonic comic relief, this scene provides a restatement of the emasculation motif. Note the Chief's comment: "What makes people so impatient is what I can't figure; all the guy had to do was wait." In other words, until Big Nurse got around to doing it for him!

THE VOTE

Structure

Another complex scene encompassing several distinct movements: we are at another Group Meeting. Actual events are cross - cut with flashbacks end fantastic connections being made by Bromden who the others think is asleep. The course of his illness and a symbolic history of his time on the Ward pass interview as the ritual progress of the Group Meeting fades in and out of his consciousness. Interspersed with shifting visions are interpretations and insights, some in symbolic form, some literal, rational. The Chief's dawning awareness of what it means to be a man is set by Kesey on a collision course with a difficult and immediate moral choice - whether to step out of the fog and help McMurphy (at a real risk to himself) or to remain hidden, safe, and hopeless. His choice is for sanity. The importance of his decision cannot be overestimated in terms of the novel's structure. It, together with McMurphy's critical choice whether to save himself or save the others (which occurs at the end of Part II), creates an inevitable current carrying all future events before it: from this moment Bromden's rebirth is certain as from the second McMurphy's fate is sealed.

Characterization

The genesis of Bromden's illness and its relation to the omnipresent fog is made crystal clear through a series of flashbacks. Fog is a part of his past, at first a neutral part. It was used to hide airfields from enemy bombers during the Second World War. On the day he landed in Europe a chemical fog protected his plane from pursuing enemy fighters and so it lodged in his subconscious as an oasis of safety. But fog had an ominous side, too; a man could get lost in it, wandering about alone and frightened without any reference points to guide him. Fog made it difficult, painful, to see, but while Bromden was still sane he understood the pain of trying was preferable to losing his bearings; it was the choice a man had to make. Bromden's sanity, uprooted the way his tribal roots had been, lost in the fog of strange airfields, was shaken further by wartime horrors he had to witness, impotently. The final blow that snapped his mind was the hollow bureaucratic ritual coexisting with and dominating the world of life and death. For a while Bromden fights his insanity, trying to see things in the fog during his first

BRIGHT NOTES STUDY GUIDE

days on the Ward, calling out for help in the form of human contact. But the institution is only nominally set up to effect cures and help the sick; its real purpose is custodial, its code, expediency. Bromden's reward for struggling is the Shock Shop, whose treatments plunge him deeper and deeper into the fog until he learns to lie low, play it cagey, keep his own counsels. Then he is safe ... but insane.

Symbolism

Four symbolic visions pass before the Chief, each one the fragment of a life, each one delivering a lesson that takes him a step closer to understanding what has happened to him and what he must do. The first life is Colonel Matterson's, overtly insane by the institution's standards which Bromden always accepted. Now he looks hard at Matterson, for the first time, and understands. The old man makes sense, a sense of his own, and other men, like Bromden, have things to learn from Matterson if only they would try. As R.D. Laing has pointed out, there is no insanity - only behavior the majority won't tolerate. But Matterson is not crazy and useless as the institution says - the institution is a liar! First lesson: figure things out for yourself! Next comes Pete Bancini's face, out of a life filled with pain, horrible effort to do the smallest thing that average men do easily. Why did he even try? Because he wanted to keep the world of men in sight; because the real world and its pain is worth more than the safety of being fogged in. The second lesson is: Live in the World of Men! Billy Bibbit's face swings into view, like a beggar's needing more than anyone can give, stuttering and whining about lost loves and lost life. Talk can't possibly reach his hurts. Third lesson: a man must try to help himself! The ghost of Bromden's father is the shell of his father, wrecked by whiskey, his aim (sharp sight) gone. But this time

Bromden sees there's nothing you can do about the past. Life is now and tomorrow, not yesterday, is the final lesson.

The Vote

The vote crystalizes the conflict between Big Nurse and McMurphy for leadership of the Ward. The day before a similar vote has led to a humiliating defeat for McMurphy - now, with only the intervention of the control - panel incident and its exemplary effect on the inmates, he calls for another vote. A second defeat would surely establish the Nurse's power beyond reach, so the vote becomes a test of McMurphy's judgment as well.

Motivation

Symbolically, the votes are pulled out of the fog by "that big red hand of McMurphy's," bandaged where it had been cut by the effort to lift the control panel. The vote is unanimous, an event which stuns both patients and staff for both realize its symbolic import. It is a vote against Big Nurse, not just a vote for watching TV. Such a defeat would be intolerable to her. With the cunning of desperation she conceives a legalistic stratagem: a majority is necessary to change Ward policy, but only half the men have voted for the change. Translated, this means that at least one of the Chronics will have to vote with the Acutes to carry the motion. But who?

Tension Resolution

When Bromden resolves the suspense by figuratively stepping out of the fog and voting with the Acutes, he acts out in a concrete fashion the resolution of the tension inherent in his characterization as well. Until this point the reader has been unsure which way his mysterious narrator was headed. Only a moment earlier Bromden had plumbed the depths of madness, begged relief from responsibility, and acted like a baby. Now he steps out of the fog to cast his lot with the world of men, blowing his cover as it were, letting himself "in for trouble." Is this his own decision or is he McMurphy's tool? The old habits die hard, "wires" are making him do it, this time guided by McMurphy instead of the Combine - but no, the Truth will not be denied. "I did it myself": he affirms - the hard - won insight of his recent bout with madness.

Appearance Vs. Reality

The Acutes appear to have won. But note that Nurse's resort to a parliamentary maneuver to invalidate the vote destroys forever the myth of the Democratic Community. Now it is Nurse who appears to have won.

VICTORY OUT OF DEFEAT

Irony

By her casual denial of a harmless request, her attempt to upset an honest vote which expressed the will of the group, and finally by her total abrogation of democratic rights, Big Nurse has brought about what the institution has worked so hard to prevent - unification of the inmates behind a leader. When the game starts, McMurphy turns the TV set on; Big Nurse, aware she is being watched, turns it off, but McMurphy remains seated, watching the blank screen. One by one the men drop their utensils, symbols of their effeminization, and take places beside McMurphy, watching the grey screen. It is an event far beyond Big Nurse's ken! She begins to lose control. The scene closes on the Chief's doubly ironic comment.

THE STAFF MEETING

Structure

This scene begins Part II, which like the final two parts is considerably shorter than Part I. Keep in mind as you read, however, that each part shares this important structural characteristic - a dramatic **climax** of great significance. Mark, too, this is the first unguarded glimpse of Big Nurse we have been given. All our information prior to this moment has been either hearsay or incomplete (inferred from her actions or speeches on the Ward). Now we see her in her own milieu.

Satire

The doctors are shown to be like children, giggling, even revealing their fears of McMurphy! The meeting is completely under domination of Big Nurse - revealing Kesey's belief that competence determines power regardless of what the titular succession appears to be.

Symbolism

Both the Head Doctor and a resident named Gideon announce their conviction that McMurphy "is no ordinary man." Big Nurse, denying this, prevents his transfer to the Disturbed Ward (and its cruciform shock table) because she fears he may be considered a martyr: again, note the Christ associations.

Prophecy

Big Nurse's prophecy will dictate the development of Part II. She demonstrates great insight into human character. McMurphy, according to her, is not an extraordinary individual, merely a self - indulgent psychopath. When he realizes his actions hold real and definite dangers to himself, he will forswear them, self - interest being dominant in his makeup. When the residents protest this will take a great deal of time, she relies on the fact that they have all the time they need - length of his commitment is at their discretion.

Characterization

The Chief has emerged from his moment of truth in scene 24, still feigning dumbness, still retaining a somewhat paranoid perspective yet somehow altered. His reasoning seems keener, his observations more acute. The quality of narrative, in fact, is quite objective compared to earlier episodes. For example, when he realizes the Nurse has survived the encounter with McMurphy and remains "strong as ever," he isn't cast into despair by the discovery, as he was in scene 17.

CANADIAN HONKERS

Characterization

After the vote and the staff meeting, Bromden watches the progress of the conflict closely, but sees no signs that McMurphy is easing up on the pressure (as Big Nurse had predicted). What he does see, however, is a deepening in the McMurphy characterization, which is to say, behaviors that complicate the character and add new dimension to him. He sees McMurphy painting pictures, writing letters "in a beautiful flowing hand," and reacting to letters he receives with concern. What Kesey seems to be saying here is that softer traits can exist in a real man; it is the balance that counts. Chief Bromden's character continues to undergo transformation. He studies himself in a mirror (sees himself), wondering that his formidable exterior can conceal such an undefined interior character, recognizing that he has always been defined by what other people wanted him to be. McMurphy, he sees, is just the opposite, all his actions "coming to him just as natural as drawing breath." By comparison and contrast Bromden gains insight into himself and McMurphy - an insight which engenders in him a new feeling of hope.

Foreshadowing

For the first time since his commitment Bromden, is able to see out of the windows into the outside world. Memories come, but they are pleasant ones. We sense that Bromden is healing, preparing to take his place back in the world of men.

Symbolism

As he watches the sky, a flight of honkers is first heard, then seen pinned against the moon - the lead goose like a great black cross in the circle of light. The flock seems to be laughing. The Chief remembers that all his efforts to kill such a goose in his youth were never successful. The symbolism is unmistakable: free things like McMurphy exist in the world in spite of every attempt to kill them and regiment life - we have only to look, to open our eyes, and they are there to see: inspirational (their flight forms a V, the World War II victory sign) and exemplary. You will recall that like the lead goose, McMurphy was first heard, then seen, by Bromden.

Motivation

A fascinating miniature at the close of this scene suggests why the institutional personnel treat the inmates with such casual cruelty. The night nurse with the purple birthmark is shown rubbing the stigmata with a crucifix to eradicate it before bed each night; upon arising she discovers it has returned like Prometheus' liver. Since she cannot even consider blaming her difficulties on herself or Fate, she must find a scapegoat: association with the sick on the Ward.

THE SWIMMING POOL

Structure

McMurphy's actions have been predicated on incomplete information and false assumptions about the extent of Big Nurse's power, a truth she had deduced by the time of the first staff meeting. In this scene he learns that "commitment," unlike a prison sentence, is indeterminate and at the discretion of authorities. The lifeguard character serves as a dramatic illustration of what this means: picked up on a drunk and disorderly charge he has been eight years and eight months (note the **allusion** to the pair of eights in the dead man's hand!) in the asylum. As Big Nurse predicted, the implications for McMurphy's freedom are instantly perceived: the risk of rebellion seems intolerable. The McMurphy character undergoes an immediate reversal.

Foreshadowing

McMurphy's shift to a self - interest motivation is neatly foreshadowed in the incident with the hydrocephalic boy. Echoing the parable of the Good Samaritan, in reverse, McMurphy refuses to respond to Harding's entreaty for help in assisting the boy. McMurphy's response is abrupt and callous, unlike the McMurphy we have seen before.

Symbolism

Water symbolism is common in literature and myth; *Cuckoo's Nest* is no exception, water symbols occurring regularly throughout. Though water is most often a significate for life, healing, regeneration and the like, it may also bear darker correspondences to death. Bromden, we learn, was "real brave" around water as a boy, but when his father began to be afraid (when the water was trapped and regulated by the hydroelectric dam), then Bromden also began to fear water.

Motivation

If McMurphy is, indeed, as the Nurse has seen him, driven by self - interest, then the dramatic change in his behavior makes very good psychological sense - the radical shift being explained by an effort of will. The change is confirmed when Cheswick, seeking redress of a grievance, appeals for McMurphy's help;

when this is refused it sends Cheswick into hysteria - resulting in his banishment to the Disturbed Ward.

CHESWICK'S DEATH

Symbolism

Cheswick commits suicide because he has allowed himself Hope - in symbolic terms, that McMurphy would Redeem him; in psychological terms, that his isolation was finally over and that he had found someone to stand beside. When McMurphy betrays that hope, Cheswick has no reason left to live - he has seen how ugly and expedient the world really is.

Analogy

The Chief draws a parallel between McMurphy's caginess, "giving in because it was the smartest thing to do," and his father's surrender to the government. Expediency is seemingly accepted as a natural element of life - but we remember the haunting echo of Cheswick's last words.

SEFELT'S SEIZURE

Symbolism

Scanlon's comment at the scene's close interprets the symbolism of the scene and suggests a parallel to McMurphy's dilemma. On the literal level, Sefelt, an epileptic, has given the medicine he needs to control his affliction to another epileptic. Behind this charitable gesture is Sefelt's fear of the side effects of the drug:

rotting gums and falling hair - a fear compounded by his pathetic belief he is losing his attractiveness to women (his masculinity). Although Big Nurse insists he take the medicine (emasculation motif), he avoids it when he can. Ironically, the effects of a seizure are equally bad, the teeth - gritting spasm causing the weakened gums to surrender their hold on the teeth. And in a double **irony**, the medicine will not prevent seizures, it simply lengthens the interval between them.

Structure

With relaxation of McMurphy's leadership the ward is returning to "normal." Kesey arranges a string of such scenes, showing the predicament of the inmates.

ONE FLEW OVER THE CUCKOO'S NEST

TEXTUAL ANALYSIS

PART IV

....

THE MECHANISM REPAIRED

Structure

A scene as brief as this one provides a sharp rhythmic contrast to the regular ebb and flow of a book - it calls attention to itself by its very brevity, like an artificially shortened line in poetry (Think of "La Belle Dame Sans Merci"). In order to harmonize and justify the attention such a scene calls to itself, it must contain matter of unusual importance. In this instance, it is the Chief's announcement that the Ward is back on schedule: Big Nurse's firm white hands are on the Controls.

HARDING'S WIFE

Theme And Motif

Harding's wife, whose large breasts serve to identify her as a younger version of Big Nurse, displays a number of the pernicious traits Kesey seems to associate with matriarchy. Like Big Nurse she emasculates, demonstrating the sharpness of her scalpel on Harding by mocking in turn, his laugh, "that mousy little squeak," his sexuality, "... you never do have enough, do you?," his friends "the hoity - toity boys," and his love. In addition, she uses her sexual desirability to gain attention and things - she takes rather than gives. (All Kesey's sympathetic women give, as RPM's mother, Bromden's grandmother, and the Disturbed Ward nurse do.) She tries to stir up sexual rivalries and contention among men by using her body, flaunting it to provoke.

Motivation

McMurphy's explosion at Harding reflects his increasing awareness of the bind he is in (as Scanlon put it); all the men on the Ward need something from him; they have seen from past events that he can help them and in spite of their understanding he fears having his commitment extended, their need cannot help but show, as it does when Harding asks McMurphy what he thinks of Mrs. Harding. Behind the innocent request is a craving for counsel and companionship, but McMurphy's fear of becoming like the lifeguard stifles his natural generosity.

Symbolism

McMurphy's dream of faces is a critical event in the regression from "himself." It is a sign of incipient insanity, recalling the visions of Bromden populated with disembodied faces hovering in the fog. To deny himself and his own generous and charitable nature, however expedient it may seem in the particular sense, spells the death of his personality. This is bitter **irony** indeed, once again recalling Scanlon's assessment of Sefelt's plight.

THE CONTROL PANEL (II)

Symbolism

The control panel which McMurphy earlier attempted to lift returns now, fraught with new meanings. We learn that it is an unused control for a hydrotherapy machine (literally: a water - healing machine!) that has no water in its nozzles. Martini is playing a childish military charade with the machine when he sees invisible people hanging in the shower harnesses waiting to be healed. McMurphy looks and sees nothing, whereupon Martini signals a re - entry of what has gradually become a new thematic element in the book, the privation and yearning of others, by saying: "Hold it a minute. They need you to see them." Notice the very subtle, inclusion of the idea of obligation rather than free choice - the overruling of protest by the injunction, "Hold it a minute." McMurphy responds again with anger, but the fact that he is moved is witnessed by his trembling hands.

THE SHOCK ROOM

Literary Technique

Cuckoo's Nest is driving toward another crescendo as the end of Part II approaches. Kesey has been preparing us for another large change in his **protagonist** by demonstrating in a succession of brief scenes how great the need for a champion is on the Ward. But the threat to McMurphy's own existence, if change back to his old self he does, is the same as it was when he decided on his previous, uncommitted, course of action. If McMurphy is to make a Hero's Decision, if McMurphy is to win Heroic Stature, he must be fully aware of the horrors that face him personally. He must see his Fate as it really is, ponder his decision, then commit himself regardless of what he knows it will cost him; to act out of incomplete knowledge or from a momentary whim would be foolhardy or stupid, reckless, not heroic. Therefore, Kesey sets his stage for the second **climax**: the Shock Shop and lobotomy are displayed before RPM with all their horrors. Brain - burning and frontal - lobe castration are the images paraded before McMurphy by Harding's skillful exposition.

Theme And Motif

In a brilliantly managed thematic reversal, we are finally made aware through a stunning revelation just whom Kesey holds ultimately responsible for "making all this mess" - who is at the root of the trouble Inside and Outside. To review the candidates thus far, we have been offered Bromden's Combine, the matriarchy, the Big Nurse, institutional brutality, regimentation, and by inference, a sort of wholesale shirking of responsibility (black boys, doctor, residents, night nurse, etc.) A new argument is uncovered bit by bit, in the course of casual conversation near the Shock Shop. Harding maintains Big Nurse is the cause of trouble on the Ward and most of the inmates agree. But McMurphy evinces doubt; at first he thought so but no more. When he is unable to explain clearly what he means, Bromden misconstrues what RPM is trying to say, assuming he has arrived at the Combine theory independently. But this curious error in judgment suddenly throws McMurphy's real point into focus. With the Chief it is the Combine, with Scanlon the Nurse, with Sefelt the drugs, with Fredrickson his family ... everybody gripes constantly, displacing responsibility onto somebody else. Here is an embryonic statement of the new **theme**. But McMurphy has not sufficiently clarified the thought in his own mind - more false starts remain; however, it is certain the problem does not reside in "a bitter - icy - hearted old woman." Then where?

It takes a dramatic cataclysm to supply the answer which comes in a casual off - hand remark from Harding: he and most of the other inmates of the asylum are not committed, but are there of their own free will! All events that have transpired to this point snap into a new perspective. McMurphy is temporarily unable to comprehend this turn of events which indeed is the major turning point of the novel and absolutely essential to comprehending its nature.

McMurphy may be confused, but the reader has no difficulty now identifying the central problem of *Cuckoo's Nest* - McMurphy will be a savior all right, but it is not Big Nurse or the Combine he must save the inmates from. He correctly perceives the illusion there. No, it is themselves he must save them from, for in the words of Pogo, so exactly mirroring the heart of this book: "We has met the enemy and they is us!"

Symbolism

An intricate bit of symbolic wordplay catches another aspect of the new **theme**: McMurphy is committed, the others are not. Notice how gracefully the simple term shuttles back and forth between a literal and a figurative level.

REBIRTH

Motivation

What motivates the last critical turn in the McMurphy persona? Only a portion of it can be explained rationally. The only factor that intervenes between his announcement to Harding that he intends to swallow his pride and look out for himself and his dramatic rebellion is the discovery that the men are self - committed, nailed to crosses of their own devising. Therefore we should look there for his motivation. We have seen that suppressing his natural personality costs him dearly; he is losing his laugh, his hands tremble, he has nightmares, and so on - thus we could expect he is ready to break out at any time ... except for the fact his cherished freedom is at stake and he knows it. We know him to be a man capable of great self - control, so rage is not a sufficient explanation, (though there is provocation from Big Nurse); he is a proud man, true, but as he tells Harding, he has swallowed his pride. And since a simple gain - loss equation will not supply a sufficient reason, either, we must conclude he is acting out of motives of altruism, undertaken, deliberately, with a clear understanding of the personal cost. He has weighed his own future against the future of the others and cast his lot on their side of the scales. Historically, we know that people have made such choices, albeit not very often. Why? At this point psychological understanding breaks down or at least becomes extremely moot. But mythically the motive is no longer clouded - it is the price one pays to become a hero, a legend, or a Savior.

Literary Technique

Kesey understands well how to arrange the dramatic moment when a hero emerges from under wraps. His method is cinematic. In this moment of truth he chooses to cast McMurphy as the prototypical Western hero. (Think of Alan Ladd in "Shane," John Wayne in "True Grit," Randolph Scott in "Ride the High Country" or William Farnum in "Last of the Duanes.") The writing is superb, a self - **parody**, yet impossible to resist.

Structure

Structurally this marks the fourth and most significant step in the series of defensive postures that McMurphy has driven Ratched to assume. He has, by turns, puzzled her, angered her, and made her uncertain, but for the first time she experiences fear. The determined, masculine approach of McMurphy has her scared.

Symbolism

The exploding glass of the nurse's station bursts forth "like water splashing" ... the water of life missing from the hydrotherapy machine, not the water of death Cheswick drowned in.

THE BASKETBALL TEAM

Structure

Part III deals entirely with McMurphy's efforts to unite the inmates into a mutually reinforcing society, the main thrust being the organization and execution of a fishing trip to the Outside. To mark the progress of the men toward cooperation (and away from isolation), Kesey shows us that McMurphy, his old self again, has organized the men into a basketball team over the opposition of Big Nurse. The team practices on the Ward, a concession McMurphy wins from Dr. Spivey (again over Nurse's protest) that upsets routines.

Literary Technique

Kesey is simultaneously managing four lines of character development: McMurphy's, the Chief's, Big Nurse's, and that of the minor actors. In this scene, as throughout Part III, Kesey is amassing evidence that McMurphy's influence is beginning to change the minor characters. Dr. Spivey stands up to Big Nurse, Harding begins to flirt with the student nurses, Bibbit ceases to write in the logbook, and so on. At the same time we need a reciprocal movement from Big Nurse, for she is seen by the men as the barometer of their progress. Thus we have signs of the strain on her, as when she binds McMurphy's wound unnaturally tight - or through her surrogates, the black boys, one of whom is driven to open hostility (rejection of the Nurse's training).

Symbolism

Repeated smashing of the Station glass cuts off the vision into the Day Room. Big Nurse can no longer see her victims, although her inflexibility forces her to continue to sit in her regular spot, "just like she could still see." Bromden knows better; behind the cardboard she is "a picture turned to the wall."

THE GOVERNMENT MEN

Characterization

The Chief's flashbacks have been becoming increasingly lucid. Now we are given one which is almost completely sane in the traditional sense. The scene supplies us with a great deal of **exposition** about Bromden's boyhood and the life of the tribe, but more important, it traces the roots of his illness which we discover go far back in time. Specific elements in the later fantasies occur with sufficient clarity to make connections. The substance of the flashback deals with an aborted trip by a government team to make an offer for the tribal lands. The mission is halted by the disgust of one official with the Indian way of life and by a cunning plan devised on the spot to make the offer through Bromden's mother, a white woman from town. The architect of this plan is an older woman who reminds Bromden of Big Nurse. Dialogue detailing this plan and the appraiser's contempt for the tribe takes place within earshot of young Bromden, the team apparently unaware the boy speaks English. He addresses them directly, only to be greeted by a stunning phenomenon - not one of the party of whites acts as if they heard a thing! Suddenly he can see ... the seams where they're put together! And the apparatus inside them that hears words - but only if the words spoken have some connection with the machine's interior programming. His didn't, so the machinery disposed of them.

Symbolism

As the Chief points out, people began acting like he couldn't hear or see long before he assumed the disguise. Not just the government men, but in school, in the Army, and now in the hospital.

Analogy

The government people are like the night nurse with the purple birthmark - they dislike what is different. We see them standing on the extreme end of this continuum, pleased to be able to eradicate something different, unwilling to try to see good before they pass final judgment (a step, as we see here, taken quite casually).

Satire

The **irony** in the woman's quoting her sociology professor may be taken as a snipe at bloodless academics whose word - worlds have little effect on practical decision - making (certainly not the effect intended).

THE CHIEF SPEAKS

Literary Technique

Kesey has carefully arranged this moment; the Chief's paranoia has faded gradually and credibly as awareness of himself and his history returned. The time for speech is at hand. As narrator looking back on events, the Chief has been able to relate his tale, but not to act fully in it since dramatic characters require speech for fully realized connections with the other players. Yet he must now become a major actor in order to justify McMurphy's onrushing sacrifice, since Kesey has selected him as the principal index of his protagonist's transformational powers and the torchbearer who keeps the spirit of RPM alive. With scarcely 100 pages left, Kesey has just enough time to effect the change from Chief Broom to Chief Bromden. In the time remaining the Indian must display courage, strength, understanding, and altruism if we are to accept him as the successor - Hero needed for a satisfactory resolution.

Motif

The stage is set for Bromden's emergence by another of the gratuitous acts of cruelty we have come to expect from Ward attendants. In the dead of night, Geever (perhaps an ironic play on the word giver) discovers the Chief's cache of old used chewing - gum and begins to take it. After the boy has gone, RPM begins to sing one of his characteristic songs, this one poking a little fun at the whole business of the dried - out treasure. The Chief is furious, but in spite of himself begins to see the humor in the situation. Laughter wells up inside him, not at the singing, but at his own foolishness.

Symbolism

Symbolically, the act that startles Bromden into speech is a gift from McMurphy of a pack of gum. Geever has indicated that no one, not ever the Red Cross lady, ever gave Bromden anything before. His first words are "thank you," an acknowledgment we must take to cover all that McMurphy has done for Bromden, not simply the gift of chewing gum.

Literary Technique

We get a fascinating glimpse behind the curtains of a writer's stage in this scene as we discover an inconsistent detail which has survived the editing process. McMurphy is seen with a panther tattoo on his shoulder, yet we know from scene 11 that his two shoulder tattoos consist of a red - eyed devil and a poker hand.

Analogy

An important part of the ensuing conversation between McMurphy and Bromden is the analogy drawn between Bromden's "invisibility" in the episode of the government men and a similar incident that took place in McMurphy's life at approximately the same age. McMurphy's response to being ignored by the beanpickers he worked with as a boy was to create an enormous ruckus. The incident cost him a bonus but his assessment is that it was worth it. In other words: It was worth paying a price to be heard!

Allusion

As the Chief reviews the destruction of his father by his mother and the townspeople, he becomes extremely agitated. When McMurphy cautions him to "cool it for a while," he notices that his bed is hot. The **allusion** is to Ahab's bed in *Moby Dick* (actually, his pillow) which Dough - Boy the steward finds "frightful hot," a sign, in Stubb's eyes, of a conscience at work.

Foreshadowing

The Chief's insight that he has been "talking crazy" signals the giant strides he will continue to take toward complete recovery for the balance of the book. Once again the control panel returns as the center of a fateful bargain between McMurphy and the Chief. McMuphy gives Bromden his solemn word he will restore his strength to him, if the Chief promises to lift the panel.

CAPTAIN GEORGE

Symbolism

Big George the Water Freak, we recall, was the only inmate on the Ward to refuse McMurphy's handshake in scene 3. Furthermore he is a Chronic, not an Acute, and hence more difficult to reach. When McMurphy is able to prevail upon this most difficult case to join the team he reaches an important milestone in his labor. That he is able to bring George's conversation out of fantasy into reality is a sign of the healing effect he is having.

Characterization

As McMurphy's actions gain more and more metaphorical valence, Kesey must take pains to ground his story on the literal level, to keep his protagonist from becoming what he has satirized earlier a symbol for literary majors to argue about. Notice how skillfully he deflates possible pretensions about McMurphy in the encounter just mentioned. The symbolic assertion, "We need you, George," is immediately followed by the refreshingly crass "You got ten bucks, by the way?"

THE EXPEDITION

Structure

This moderately long scene is almost equally divided into an Inside (the asylum) and an Outside section. The regenerative effect of McMurphy is prominent inside the asylum, form the mock - serious suicide of the machines upon Candy's entrance onto the Ward, to the more tangible evidences of recovery: Bibbit's sexual bravado, Ellis' removing the nails from his own hands to wish Billy well, and the Doctor's decision to come along, incidentally saving the entire healing expedition and frustrating Big Nurse's design to squelch the trip.

Foreshadowing

A dark element in the preparations which goes almost unnoticed is Big Nurse's public declaration that McMurphy is profiting by the trip. This seed of doubt about McMurphy's motives in general will come to flower in Part IV.

Complications

The Outside portion of the journey is structured in an interesting fashion. The self - confidence built up on the Inside must be tested on the Outside if we are to acknowledge that McMurphy's magic is really working. Therefore a current of doubt is introduced into the proceedings. Once free of the cuckoo's nest, the uniformed inmates become aware of the gawking contempt of passersby. Bromden restates the pain - of - manhood **theme**. By main force, joking, storytelling, toughness, cunning and courage McMurphy carries his twelve disciples through the obstacles the Outside places between them and the life - giving sea. The townspeople serve as barriers that complicate McMurphy's task - to lead the men to the ocean.

Symbolism

The fatal course McMurphy is embarked upon is signified by the recurrence of the double - 8 motif, the low pair in the dead man's hand tattooed across his muscle. The motif appears in the form of a statistic illustrating the need for oil filters, but today McMurphy is not buying.

THE COMBINE'S WORK

Theme And Motif

Bromden confesses the men still have not been able to laugh, acknowledging they will not be truly strong until they can see a funny side to things.

Characterization

Bromden asks himself a crucial question about McMurphy - is it possible he works on the funny side of life so much because he can't see the painful side? If this were true, it would, of course, rob McMurphy of his nobility and his actions of any Heroism.

Satire

Bromden professes to see the Combine at work in the changes he witnesses in the Outside. His examples are clues to a rational conception of the evil force of his paranoid fantasies.

Foreshadowing

Unlike McMurphy, the Acutes are going to get out of the cuckoo's nest alive and well, thanks to his sacrifice. Harding foreshadows this pass in the last line of the scene.

LAUGHTER

Theme And Motif

The tension of the expedition, heightened by the last - minute possibility that Captain Block would prevent the Lark (a happy bird) from sailing, complicated by the humiliating treatment of the dock mob, is replaced by sea, sky, and sun, the healing forces of Nature, and then by a much different form of tension than the men have experienced in years: the excitement of a salmon run. The absurdity of the situation causes McMurphy to boom his mighty laugh around the boat, infecting Harding, then Scanlon, Candy, Sefelt, the Doctor ... and all. The inmates are becoming men.

Characterization

McMurphy, who has single - handedly kept the expedition together, suddenly refuses a request for help during the salmon run. Literally everyone, even the Doctor, is calling for his assistance to boat fish, but he remains aloof, laughing. When the men realize he is telling them to help themselves they find they have indeed grown enough under his tutelage to get the job done without assistance.

The **theme** of self - reliance as well as the laughter motif is thus realized in this scene. Answering the crucial question he asked in the last scene, Bromden sees that McMurphy does understand life's painful side, "but he won't let the pain blot out the humor no more'n he'll let the humor blot out the pain."

A SEA CHANGE

Transformation

The men who return to the dock are not the boys who left it. Sparked by the boldness of their voyage, the self - reliance it has entailed, and the laughter it has provoked, they have proved they can brave the terrors of Outside. George proves a magnificent Captain, the doctor has landed a strange and enormous monster fish, Billy Bibbit volunteers his life jacket to the girl when they discover the boat is short of jackets. Captain Block and the police await the arrival but instead of cringing, "the doctor carried the fight to them," causing them to back off. In stark contrast with their humiliating sendoff, this time the dock loafers have nothing to say.

Appearance And Reality

George, the water freak, turns out to have captained a PT boat in the Pacific and holds the Navy Cross. Kesey is telling us, as he has throughout, that we must look beyond surfaces when we measure a man.

Foreshadowing

Near shore a storm is brewing, an indication that McMurphy's "boat ride" is nearly over.

Symbolism

McMurphy insists on returning to his boyhood home ("a good home") on the way back to the asylum. One of the enduring elements of heroic myth, the return home before a climactic battle, it serves to allow the hero to draw strength from his roots and make his farewells, enabling him to face his impending doom with courage. As a testimonial to his endurance, the symbol of his first sexual encounter, a girl's dress, is still flying in the wind, partially intact, from a tree where it was blown many years earlier. Recognizing that Love has been the main thematic strain of his existence, McMurphy tells us "it's the God's truth."

The Vampire Metaphor

A number of ominous signs warn us that McMurphy is fast losing his strength. As in the Christian mystery of Communion (where a wafer and wine do not represent, but Are, the body and blood of Christ), he is doling out his own life for the others to live. After the trip, the Acutes appear "red - cheeked" and "full" while McMurphy is "beat" "wornout," "exhausted" and, most tellingly, pale. Harding explains it as the loss of a suntan, but we know better; it is the men who are draining him of vital force. Bromden observes him straining to maintain appearances, but looking "dreadfully tired." McMurphy is in a race between his own waning strength and the needs of the men to achieve full salvation - a point they have not as yet reached. His understanding of this gives him a frantic quality.

ONE FLEW OVER THE CUCKOO'S NEST

THE GROUP MEETING

Motivation

As Part IV begins, Miss Ratched is ready to undertake another offensive against McMurphy. Recognizing that McMurphy's altruistic strain is extremely rare in human experience, but that it is an often assumed disguise of charlatans, she sets about to plant seeds of doubt among his followers: her main tool being an attack on the credibility of his motivation as saint or martyr. Through her rhetorical skill, the men are forced to a mutually exclusive set of choices - he is either a saint or a con man motivated by self interest. What Ratched in effect has done is to force the men to see McMurphy as a caricature instead of a rounded individual. No such either/or choice really describes humanity; it is possible to share characteristics of both modes (altruistic and self - serving), and in fact most of us do.

Appearance And Reality

Of the two caricature poles offered, con man or saint, the men are driven in spite of themselves to choose the former, since McMurphy's general manner is seemingly inconsistent with the latter position. Once again Kesey has found a way to tell us that what seems to be is often at odds with what is, that people make little effort to look beyond surfaces.

Literary Technique

At all times Kesey is under obligation to maintain his literal tale as well as his allegory. Harding's speech about capitalism, which explains McMurphy's actions as self - serving but grounded in a respectable, even praise worthy economic philosophy in which almost anything goes if no attempt is made to conceal one's rapacious motives, is satirical, but meant seriously as well. Here is a framework which (apparently!) preserves McMurphy's good - guy image, yet explains his behavior without resort to mysticism. The fact that there seem to be some holes in Harding's analysis is explained by him as simply meaning that McMurphy is clever enough to keep the totality of his design obscure.

Characterization

Scene 43 offers an ironic measure of just how far the Chief has progressed toward normality. Although he still believes in

McMurphy as "a giant come out of the sky to save us," he is swayed by the other men's analysis until he comes "halfway to thinking like the others" about McMurphy's motives. The tub room **episode** where Bromden finally lifts the control - panel and causes the inmates to lose their bets to McMurphy carries him the other half of the way. He refuses McMurphy's token of appreciation and accuses his friend of always maneuvering things to his own advantage.

Irony

Bromden, almost sane now and able to participate in Ward life, his giant strength returned to him - all as McMurphy had promised, is not elated by the transformation and grateful, but rather critical of his benefactor. His moral judgment reminds us of the old proverb about looking gift horses in the mouth or Marc Antony's reproach: "The evil men do lives after them; the good is oft 'terred with their bones ..."

THE SHOWER

Structure

The plot makes its last turn as McMurphy's status on the Ward changes permanently. With the attack on Washington in the shower room there will be no turning back from events that rush McMurphy forward to the sacrifice.

Revelation

Kesey's problem for some time has been to discover a way to identify McMurphy's saintly altruism to the inmates without breaking the logic of the characterization - a symbolic piece of action wherein his true nature is revealed so that he may escape the invidious comparison with con men (or even with shrewd capitalism!).

The revelation comes when he steps in to prevent brutalization of George at the hands of his Nemesis, Washington. There is no way to reconcile the con man image of self - service with the fatal step McMurphy takes. His true nature is unmistakably revealed in that moment to the inmates.

Heroic Motivation

McMurphy holds aloof as long as he does, even allowing Washington the first two punches, because he is totally aware of the irrevocability of the step he is about to take and its deadly consequences.

Inevitability

The encounter of force between McMurphy and Washington, McMurphy and Big Nurse, and McMurphy and the system (Combine, "East," Institute) has been inevitable from the first day of McMurphy's admission. The choices he appeared to have were only illusory; because of the nature of the character he is, he is compelled to act as he does in the shower scene and afterward. As Bromden tells us, he approaches the fight with "helpless, cornered despair," not out of physical fear but because he is aware he is powerless to alter his own destiny. Such inevitability in a plotline is a quality rarely achieved in the various forms of fiction - when it is it is taken as one of the parameters that mark the presence of a literary artist.

THE DISTURBED WARD

Allusion

Although the entire scene is laced with Christian symbolism, the most important reference is to Christ's opportunity to escape the Cross by denying he is the Son of God. Christ's Agony and Death then become his own choice, not the imposition of some external authority. McMurphy is offered a chance to escape the cruciform EST table if he will accept guilt for disturbing Nurse's world and acknowledge (figuratively) that Washington had a right to torment George (deny the legitimacy of his savior's role).

Analogy

In an obvious analogy to a well - known custom of Chinese prison camps whereby a prisoner is asked to sign a written confession, including a statement of how well he has been treated, McMurphy sarcastically requests such a paper to sign from Big Nurse. In spite of the fact that a signed confession wasn't literally what she has come for, her instinctive response is to comply with the request - illustrating that the correspondence McMurphy has seen is more than circumstantial.

Characterization

After being driven back, temporarily, into fantasy and fog by the shock treatment, the Chief discovers an anchor to clutch which saves him from regression into the sick animal we met at the novel's outset. It is McMurphy's final advice to Bromden, delivered with McMurphy's indomitable wink - "Guts ball." The expression, taken from sports jargon, refers to situations where there is no hope of victory in terms of the score; yet, if one undertakes his obligation to play against towering odds, he will earn a moral victory nonetheless, a victory over himself!

Deliverance

Bromden's willingness to fight, to try and hold out against the shock, is the dramatic test of McMurphy's gospel. Bromden announces that he will never again hide in the fog. This time he works at coming out of the shock effect and succeeds. In terms of the conflict statements of *Cuckoo's Nest* this is a major victory and Bromden sees it as such.

THE PARTY

Structure

When McMurphy emerges from the systematic shock treatments, the rational and literal part of him understands that he must escape from the asylum or die. His purpose appears safely achieved, the Acutes are well on the way to manhood and deliver guarantees they will sign themselves out of the Ward shortly. Chief Bromden tells him he, too, will escape shortly after McMurphy. Big Nurse stands discredited, having blasted his brain with thousands of volts of electricity to no apparent avail. The resolution of plot tensions seems at hand. McMurphy therefore has no reason to remain and he agrees with the Acutes that he must clear out. Their willingness to assist his escape can be taken as the final evidence of the sane personality change they have undergone - for in the novel's terms the concern for another is taken as the highest good, proof positive of well being.

Irony

The party which prevents McMurphy from leaving at the moment of his triumph is to lead directly to his destruction, a far cry from the outcome he and the others expect. In a prescient moment rich in ironic **foreshadowing** he says "... let's say maybe it's my going away party."

Symbolism

In remaining behind when mortal danger threatens, McMurphy underrates the Nurse's strength and tenacity. "I've took their worst shot," he is to say after the carnage of the affair is discovered by Big Nurse, rejecting a final desperate bid at escape. This lapse in judgment, growing out of McMurphy's pride in his accomplishments, tells us we are in the presence of the sin of hubris, an extreme form of self - confidence that the Ancients considered a sin against the Gods, only they being entitled to such utter confidence in their own invincibility.

Literary Technique

The party itself is the **climax** of McMurphy's efforts to unify the men and bring them the gift of boldness and laughter. Although the scene has been criticized as lacking the tightness and economy of the other parts of *Cuckoo's Nest*, and though its constituent incidents appear somewhat forced, lacking the inevitable motivation we have come to expect from Kesey, still the scene serves as a capstone for an important section of McMurphy's theorizing. A party is, after all, an occasion where restraints are removed and abandon dominates. Even a conventional morality holds, however reluctantly, that the better the party the more it is characterized by abandon. High spirits, then, are the final sign the inmates are capable of participating fully in life, giving themselves up to it without the caution "Combine" conditioned robots would exercise.

Foreshadowing

At a high point in the party's action, Harding, in a drunken **parody** of priesthood, delivers a prophecy which will prove true - for McMurphy: "You are witnessing the end .... We are doomed ..."

THE END OF THE PARTY

Characterization

Throughout the party we have seen evidences, large and small, that McMurphy's presence on the Ward has done its intended work. The most dramatic change, apart from the Chief's is in Harding - who proves forceful and decisive in organizing the "escape" for McMurphy. Bromden, recognizing RPM's drunkenness and extreme fatigue, says of Harding, "I was glad he was there to take over." When McMurphy asks Harding to help him to understand what makes cuckoo's nests, Harding replies thoughtfully and with wisdom, proving his accession to insight about himself. In his case it was Guilt, Shame, Fear, and Self - Belittlement (the Control Tools of Miss Ratched).

THE AFTERMATH

Inevitability

Bromden sounds the thematic note of predetermined Fate once again as he comments that after giving the whole matter of the party a great deal of thought, he believes the tragic results that came in its wake would have happened anyway, even if McMurphy had escaped and Big Nurse hadn't caught Billy with the whore.

The Betrayal

Billy Bibbit's hysterical lie that McMurphy compelled him to sleep with the girl functions not only as a betrayal of McMurphy, but as a self - betrayal, too. The motivation for this reversal is sound. Kesey has prepared us for it in scene 46 with the intriguing interruption of the narrative movement prefaced by Bromden's "You have to know about Billy Bibbit," a direct characterization occupying a substantial amount of space and unlike any that has preceded. What Kesey has shown us is how deep the roots of Fear, Self - Loathing, and most of all, boyhood run in Bibbit. Under the Nurse's skillful ministrations Billy's veneer of thin manhood is stripped away together with any chance he will ever grow up. It is this last, not just the shame he feels at letting McMurphy down, that precipitates his suicide.

Theme And Motif

As McMurphy's saga draws to a close, a number of thematic elements is resolved. Big Nurse attempts to lay the burden of guilt for Bibbit's suicide on McMurphy, accusing him of thinking He Is God, an accusation which causes McMurphy to completely lose control of himself. He assaults her (this parody of a woman) in a queer **parody** of a sexual attack. And though the act is the act of a crazy man, McMurphy is strangely calm while he goes about the mad business. Another of Bromden's speculations, that McMurphy has been trapped into his course of action by the enormous, naked need of the inmates preying on his generous spirit, is brought to fruition in the penultimate scene. Once again the Chief encloses his statement in a powerful **metaphor** - this time of McMurphy as a zombie, obeying orders beamed at him by the inmates. Bromden's realization reminds us of the philosophic tenet that man creates his own gods, the gods that he needs.

ONE FLEW OVER THE CUCKOO'S NEST

Symbolism

After lobotomy, the husk of McMurphy is murdered by Bromden in a physical simulation of the act of love. Bromden thus carries out, in death, the love motif that McMurphy lived by. In addition, the murder is literally an act of love: love for the memory of the vital giant who is no more and love for his teachings which Fear would silence if Big Nurse were allowed to "use it as an example of what can happen if you buck the system." In discharging his obligation to McMurphy, Chief Bromden regains the last part of his long lost Manhood - McMurphy's promise has been kept. As McMurphy appeared to Bromden in the beginning, soaring above the cuckoo's nest, so now Bromden feels as if it is he who is flying.

Regeneration

Some critics have found Despair at the end of *One Flew Over the Cuckoo's Nest*; McMurphy is dead, Big Nurse is still in charge of the Ward, the Chief is fleeing as a fugitive, and the mysterious force that wrings the juice from modern life, whether it be called the Combine, the institution, or whatever, has hardly suffered a mortal blow. But we see the novel from quite another perspective: McMurphy has fulfilled a noble destiny and lives on in the lives he has salvaged. The drama we have witnessed is an object lesson in how to deal with the Combine - with Resistance, Persistence, Love and Laughter. We have learned not to scorn the small personal triumph which is the glorious answer to the plaintive query, "What can I do?" Big Nurse herself cannot return to her inhuman mask. It is not so much, as another critic has pointed out, that her voice is temporarily lost. That will return. But she can never again know when another McMurphy will come for her with his heels ringing sparks from the tile. Educate your enemy, don't kill him, for he is worth more alive to you than dead, said Che Guevara in his manual for revolution.

McMurphy has educated Big Nurse in responsibility. Finally, the Chief may end up exiled to Canada, but first he plans to return home and see if the rumors he heard that the tribe hasn't disintegrated are true. If they have kept the old ways alive in spite of all attempts to eradicate them, then perhaps the invincibility of the Combine is only a myth, and as McMurphy's example argued - the enemy is the force within yourself that makes you want to give up. It remains to be seen. What Bromden does know for certain is that it is high time he returned to the world of men.

ONE FLEW OVER THE

CUCKOO'S NEST

Kesey's talent in developing three central characters - McMurphy, Big Nurse, and the Chief - is one of our main concerns in Textual Analysis, Christ Metaphor, and Essay Questions. Here we shall be concerned with another facet of Kesey's talent: his ability to create a large cast of minor characters, thirty - six in all, yet each one distinct and memorable.

BANCINI

Pete has been in the condition of a Chronic all his life although he has not spent his life on the Ward. Rather he has led a useful and productive life and thus he serves as Kesey's vehicle of contrast to the others. Pete always did his job well, making up for lack of intelligence with "main force and gutpower." When Pete sees things at all he sees them quite clearly, unlike the intellectual Harding. His example puts the childish self - indulgence of the other inmates in perspective - a fact not completely lost on them and they feel vaguely ashamed in his presence.

BIG GEORGE

Note the symbolism in his obsession with sanitation. He avoids close human contact assiduously and is the only inmate not to shake McMurphy's hand upon the latter's admission. No one knows of George's earlier accomplishments and no one cares to spend the time to find out who and what the old man was on the Outside. It is only when McMurphy lays his hand on George that he begins to speak audibly again - and his words make sense! George takes charge of the Lark, acquitting himself well on the difficult crossing of the bar. Later, when the black boys tease him, McMurphy and Bromden step forward to pay their respects to George's different but evident dignity.

BILLY BIBBIT

Kesey characterizes Billy by his uncontrollable stutter and his equally uncontrollable low opinion of himself, his philosophy being: "What does it matter, nothing can ever be done, anyway." Billy is still a child; though resenting his mother and being somewhat aware of the deleterious effects of her influence (as Harding is of his wife's), he is chained to her skirts with links of steel. Next to Chief Bromden, Billy represents McMurphy's greatest challenge in the resurrection of the inmates; as Bromden is his exemplary success, Bibbit is his exemplary failure. The roots of dependency run too deeply in Billy to be uprooted even by McMurphy. John Barsness, the critic, calls him a "tragicomic figure," driven to suicide by the "healers," a man who cures himself for a brief moment by trusting his instincts, then surrenders to the "cure" of death to escape their vengeance for his presumption.

Billy's mother is a prime symbol of the matriarchy, the measure of her success being Billy's eternal "boy" ness.

BLACK BOYS

Five black "boys" appear in the novel, all Ward attendants. Although they have names and some attempt to individually characterize them is made, their important aspect is as a group. The day - shift boys especially are the black dogs of Nurse Ratched's Hell, snapping at the inmates' heels, carrying out, in an intentional, malevolent form, the more impersonal hatred of life represented by Big Nurse and the Combine. In their functions as minions of the institution and extensions of Ratched, they provide targets for McMurphy's opposition. It is a violent encounter with one of them that leads directly to McMurphy's transfer to Disturbed and the EST table. Their caricaturization as stereotypical white - hating blacks is partially justified by Kesey in the case of the dwarf (we are meant to generalize this incident in various fashions to all the attendants) who was forced to witness his mother's rape by white men. This motivation is extraneous to their actual use as character in the novel and may be taken as a form of self - defense by Kesey against racist charges. The night boys, while less poisonous than their day counterparts, represent a subtler form of institutional sadism - what one might term a casually considered or even an unconsidered variety, without conscious malice. Thus we are shown the spectacle of Geever scraping away the treasured hoard of gum the Chief, an indigent, has amassed and which constitutes his main visible source of pleasure. Said scraping is done with gleeful amusement in the dead of night, the prospect of the Indian's discomfiture adding fuel to the flames of Geever's enjoyment. His attempt to hide his real motives behind the mask of institutional cant about cleanliness being a twenty - hour job serves to emphasize the corrupt ethics of bureaucratized life.

CAPTAIN BLOCK

Kesey memorably differentiates him by giving him a bald head like the gun - turret on a U - boat. Unwilling to take his boat to sea without a waver of responsibilities from "the proper authorities," Block resembles a number of other minor characters who dislike risk and responsibility.

CHESWICK

He is an embryonic McMurphy figure, embodying McMurphy's resistance motif without being able to sustain his opposition to anything. During McMurphy's ascendancy in the Ward (Part I), Cheswick begins to firm as a character, standing up to Big Nurse in Group Meeting. When his mentor betrays the imitation by backing off the conflict with Ratched and playing it "cagey," however, Cheswick is left dangling. Rather than return to being a blustering fool, and unable to continue growing without RPM's model, Cheswick must destroy himself. Cheswick is a fine example of Kesey's ability to dramatize life's complexity even in minor characters.

COLONEL MATTERSON

He has been committed by his wife who doesn't want to take care of him any longer (although we may infer he "took care of" her for most of her adult life). Colonel Matterson's illness manifests itself in a fascinating syndrome: he sees the literal world in mysterious metaphors. Matterson is a man who makes his own kind of sense, a threat to no one, yet who is intolerable to "normal" society, because they refuse either to attempt to see what he is driving at - or conversely, to leave him alone. Although his service to the Establishment may be thought to have earned him a decent, dignified retirement, crazy or not, we see, through the agency of Matterson, that the Combine owes no loyalty or reward to anyone, including its own servants.

DR. SPIVEY

Kesey sums up Spivey's character by making him a little man with a big forehead and tiny eyes. He is another of the "intellectuals" that Kesey treats with disdain as men of theories who have no answers to the problems of the real world. Dr. Spivey's particular hobbyhorse is his Theory of the Therapeutic Community which he trots out for Group Meetings, his only real contact with the men on the Ward. This "theory," describing the way Dr. Spivey envisions his expertise actually working to heal sick minds, is exposed quickly as claptrap. It is Big Nurse, not Dr. Spivey, who in fact determines Ward policy and attitudes, a truth which emerges unmistakably from their early interaction and from staff meeting. With McMurphy's ultra - masculine example around as a model, the character of Spivey undergoes a gradual change, becoming firmer and more self - reliant. Kesey uses Spivey in part to illustrate that the effects of matriarchy are no respecters of intellect, position or income; a specific like RPM is necessary to counteract the radical personality imbalance that too much female influence induces in a man. Spivey also represents a vicious type of innocence, sinning by omission against the helpless souls whose well - being he is charged with.

ELLIS

He is a **parody** Christ, a catatonic forever frozen in crucifixion against the Ward wall, rising out of a puddle of his own urine. The staff made a "mistake" in the Shock Shop and murdered his brain. Ellis is thus a live warning to McMurphy what a dangerous game he is involving himself in.

FACTORY GIRL

A pathetic and desperate character, recently trapped in a factory job that she is aware will soon turn her youthful vitality into robotlike mechanism. A number of the minor characterizations like this one seem to point to the idea that it is the nature of the modern world, not the inherent nature of man, that drives us away from life toward mindless regimentation.

GAS STATION ATTENDANT

He is analogous on the Outside to the black boys on the Inside. His hate and contempt for the weak is near the surface, in his sneering tone of voice, his indifferent service, and his overt attempt to chisel a few dollars by pushing junk merchandise. Although Dr. Spivey and the inmates are cowed by his aggression, McMurphy understands the type very well and how to handle it.

GOVERNMENT MEN

Actually two men and a woman, sent to appraise the Columbia Indian lands and make an offer to the tribe. Physically unpleasant in appearance (the woman is reminiscent of Big

Nurse) themselves, they hold the Indian way of life in contempt. They are puffed up with self - importance and their own thin, expertise, but actually their abysmal ignorance is evident. Their casual attitude toward the serious business they are involved in echoes the attitude of the Ward personnel. It reminds us, too, of the easy cruelties of wives who behave as Mrs. Matterson, Mrs. Ruckley, or Mrs. Harding do; of developers who skin the land to erect "Nests in the West"; and of all the figuratively deaf and blind functionaries who can neither hear nor see.

GRANDMA

One of the few completely sympathetic female characters in *Cuckoo's Nest*. If we are to understand how she differs from the other female characterizations of the book, we should see that first and foremost she is a "giver" while the others are "takers." This value system is extended to the male characterizations and determines who is treated gracefully by Kesey and who is not.

HARDING, DALE

Carefully developed by Kesey, he passes from a condition of effeminate impotency through a growth, influenced by McMurphy, in which he becomes both decisive and insightful. At the novel's conclusion he has acquired some of McMurphy's expressions, his leadership in gaming, and the beginnings of a McMurphian sexuality. Harding figures in a number of key scenes, from the start serving as spokesman for what might be called an intellectual posture: aloof, slightly scornful, burying the simplicities of moral vision in a torrent of wordsounds. Harding is filled with self - loathing and guilt, his real ticket of admission to the cuckoo's nest. The genesis of this (although Kesey leaves the area ambiguous) is apparently in some homosexual experiences he has taken part in as a school boy, the results of which scar him and lead directly to overcompensation in the form of marriage to an attractive, highly sexual woman, his intellectual inferior. Vera Harding has little use for her husband beyond the need to belittle him. Together with the Big Nurse's influence she is the guarantee that he will remain in a permanent state of crippled, impotent shame, a fact he senses and resents but is helpless to combat. Harding's characterization of himself as a diseased rabbit is the metaphorical parameter of his insanity. Harding also serves to present necessary **exposition** to the reader which Bromden could not be logically expected to know, e.g., his concise essay on electroshock therapy and lobotomy. Kesey signals Harding's character in his dainty expressive hands that embarrass him.

JOEY FISH - IN - A - BARREL

One of the Indians involved in the cash settlement for lands used in the hydroelectric dam project, he owns three Cadillacs but cannot drive. Thus he illustrates in concrete terms the bad bargain foisted on the Indian, the Cadillacs being hardly better than the white man's glass beads used to purchase Manhattan island.

/4 Little Jap Nurse.

A sympathetic portrait. Her behavior is marked by the humanity that is sorely lacking in the other institutional personnel We see her, like the whores, as another of Kesey's "giving" women.

MARTINI

He can "see" things that other people cannot, often the actual essence or history of a situation dramatized for him but invisible to others. Kesey uses Martini as a kind of shaman who "sees" the needs of the group in mythic terms.

MARY LOUISE BROMDEN

One of Kesey's matriarchal figures. Her effect on her son, Chief Bromden, is summed up in his metaphoric memory of her domination: his father had been the biggest Indian in the state, but as the years passed, Bromden thought of his mother as twice as big as his father. Kesey probably means us to understand that Mary's influence on the young Chief preconditioned him to Big Nurse's tyranny.

MRS. BIBBIT

Another of Kesey's variations on the matriarchal figure. She treats her son like an adolescent boy, babying him, flirting with him, and denying the advancing years that reduce his prospects for marriage, family, career, any sort of life, in fact, other than that as her "boy."

NURSE FLINN

Kesey portrays her as Ratched's understudy, preparing for a career of inhumanity in the service of the institution.

NURSE PILBOW

She is a bundle of fears and resentments, mostly directed toward the inmates whom she has somehow associated with her disfigurement. Her demeanor strongly satirizes the traditional image of "angel of mercy" borne by her profession.

OLD BLASTIC

Kesey uses him, the oldest "Vegetable," to typify the end - product of the Combine's neglect. His life is devoid of meaning. When he dies, his body is processed out like a broken machine, attended by no human regrets or memories.

OLD RAWLER

Kesey uses him as another warning to McMurphy of what happens to a man who runs afoul of Big Nurse. Rawler's suicide by castration is symbolic of the Institutional Castration all of Big Nurse's victims must ultimately suffer.

PUBLIC RELATIONS MAN

Tagged by Kesey as a man with laugh and hands so wet you can "hear" them, the Public Relations Man is a professional liar, hired to deceive good citizens into believing the Institution is a fine place and that the society they represent is doing an excellent job on the unfortunates placed in its care. He figures in the Chief's fantasies as an ambiguously - sexed individual wearing a corset - a product of the matriarchy and the Combine

- who has no connection with real life. As a representative of the "sane," Outside he becomes a parameter against which insanity of the inmates can be measured.

THE RESIDENTS

The young medicos at the staff meeting are, like the government men and the Public Relations Man, puffed up with self - importance and pipe smoke. They are deft with jargon and polysyllables but obviously, like their leader Dr. Spivey, have little touch with the real world, little true expertise, and little concern for anything but their careers, images, and safety. Together with Dr. Spivey they add up to a power vacuum which Big Nurse has moved into.

RUCKLEY

Another staff "mistake," like Ellis, Ruckley, is now a fumbling, drooling wreck whose sole remaining words are a venomous judgment on womankind; "Ffffffffuck da wife!". One is left to speculate what horrible memory is powerful enough to force its way through the tangled mess of a botched lobotomy in this fashion.

SCANLON

An apparently normal man in most respects, Scanlon's fixation is bombing and violence. He is considered insane, of course. Yet we realize, on reflection that his preference for explosive response has been a normal characteristic of governments and men for centuries.

SEFELT AND FREDERIKSON

A grotesque Jack Sprat and wife combination, Sefelt and Frederikson are epileptics who have formed a partnership doomed to frustration. Sefelt's dilemma, a classical "double bind" or "damned if you do and damned if you don't" predicament, serves to emphasize McMurphy's developing conflict between self - interest and self - sacrifice.

TABER, MAXWELL WILSON

Another example of the kind of revenge the Combine can perpetrate on a non - conformist, he is the "Mis - tur Tay - bur" of Big Nurse's revery. Lobotomized, he became "adjusted" to the world, a complete conformist!

TEE AH MILLATOONA

(The Pine - That - Stands - Tallest - on - the - Mountain). Chief Bromden's father, who lives completely in Bromden's recollections and fantasies. An understanding of his father is one of the central levers Bromden needs access to in order to propel himself back to sanity. Tee Ah Millatoona, Chief of the Columbia Indians, is the tower of strength who holds his people together against the corrosive effects of the townspeople's scorn, a changing way of life, and the temptation of a large government purchase price for the Indian lands and fishing waters. For a while his opposition is successful but he has not reckoned on the enemy within, his white wife, who shames and demeans him, refusing to take his name and bestowing her own on his son. The old Chief, like so many characters in this novel, is a victim of man - hating matriarchy.

UNCLE HALLAHAN

One of the influences from McMurphy's past from whom he has learned something, McMurphy will not share the crucial details which he keeps a secret. As befits the comic - myth side of his nature, McMurphy has "secret powers."

UNCLE JULES

Kesey differentiates this inmate as one who was always up first in the morning because he had a theory about the timing of Evil.

UNCLE R & J WOLF

Like Bromden's lawyer uncle, Running and Jumping Wolf exists to show the lie to Indian stereotypes, in this case the myth of the stolid somber Indian. Uncle R & J Wolf is capable of rolling on the ground in an uncontrollable fit of laughter when a good joke is played on some white men.

VERA HARDING

Like Ratched, her weapon is innuendo. In her brief visit to the Ward she manages, almost simultaneously, to indicate her husband's inadequacies, suggest he is homosexual, suggest she is sleeping around, attempt to entice McMurphy, and to titillate the inmates with glimpses of deep cleavage. Her grammatical usage indicates she is relatively unlettered, a weakness Mr. Harding exploits to counterattack and salvage scraps of his dignity with. She is still another variation of the woman who emasculates men.

THE WHORES

Four females of a sexually liberal persuasion make various appearances in *Cuckoo's Nest*: Candy and Sandy of the fishing trip and party, and two unnamed young ladies from McMurphy's past, ages nine and fifteen. While each of the characterizations is different, the "whores" may be taken collectively as illustrating a type of woman that Kesey likes and admires, which stands in stark contrast to the other women of the book. What unites the girls here are the characteristics of freedom, spontaneity, generosity, humor, willingness to take risks, joy in the physical side of life. Like Bromden's grandmother, they are "givers" instead of "takers."

ONE FLEW OVER THE CUCKOO'S NEST

ESSAY QUESTIONS AND ANSWERS

. . . .

Question: Thomas Wolfe quotes Kesey as saying, "Big Nurse killed President Kennedy." What does he mean?

Answer: It is obvious that he doesn't mean his literary creation pulled the trigger on Oswald's rifle. Nor does he mean that, given an extension of *Cuckoo's Nest* in time, until the assassination day was reached, he would then have written a part as sniper for Big Nurse. What he is attempting to do is to communicate some form of truth as he sees it through the device of paradox - a statement which seems contradictory or absurd but may actually be well - founded. Paradox, a rhetorical device used to gain attention, is a particular favorite of Kesey's. In *One Flew Over the Cuckoo's Nest*, the book alluded to in the statement above, Chief Bromden, the narrator, opens the tale with another paradox, saying his story is true "even if it didn't happen."

The key to unlocking the paradox lies in the metaphorical value of Big Nurse as a part of the shadowy organization of Bromden's imagination that "adjusts" things and persons on the

Outside as Nurse does on the Inside. We recall that Miss Ratched is a high officer in this group and that among her many tasks and responsibilities the primary one is to keep things running like a smooth, accurate precision - made machine; like a pocket watch with a glass back so that everything can be seen. A central part of this plan is the making of schedules which are published and rigidly adhered to. The Public Relations Man, another officer of the Combine, often brings people around to see this tidy world, for no discernible reason other than display.

Analogously, Kennedy's Dallas trip was a Public Relations creation, with little inherent meaning other than that it was on the schedule. Similarly, each of the movements inside Dallas was also rigidly scheduled, just as Big Nurse might have done. Using the schedule, an assassin would know where the President would be and at what time! Thus, rigid adherence to a pre - set plan cost Kennedy his life, and this is one meaning of Kesey's paradox.

Question: Are elements of popular culture, movies, songs, etc., incidental or central to Kesey's design in *Cuckoo's Nest*?

Answer: Although elements of popular culture appear incidental to Kesey's design in *Cuckoo's Nest*, actually they are central to the construction of his ambience, his characterizations, motivations, **imagery**, and other aspects of the novel. We recall that McMurphy, born of Frankenstein, becomes a monster to the well - ordered world of the cuckoo's nest; as his vitality wanes from the vampire - like bloodsucking of the inmates he becomes un - dead, a "moving - picture zombie" obeying orders beamed at him from his masters. In a very definite sense, it is these zombie - masters, the inmates, who launch the fatal attack on Big Nurse at the book's conclusion. Thus McMurphy, in his aspect as creature, provides a steady antagonism to Big Nurse as machine, disrupting her regulated universe, nourishing her enemies, and ultimately becoming their weapon of terror against her. In his aspect as hero, McMurphy's most telling **imagery** is drawn from the Western film and he is a gunslinger, no angel but strangely a moral force, sent up against the best the bad guys have to offer - and overwhelming odds as well. His cap moves on his head like a ten - gallon Stetson, the iron in his heels rings sparks as he walks. He is Doc Holliday against Ringo and the Clantons at the O.K. Corral; he is Rooster Cogburn against The Original Greaser Bob; in fact, he draws so many "qualities" from a rich and deep American tradition of a Big Man for a Big Land that exact analysis of the attributions would be difficult to provide. Suffice it to say that he bears the distinct hallmark of the above - named genres, like an ambulatory double - feature.

His arch - enemy, the Big Nurse, is drawn from a complementary tradition, the mechanical monster of science - fiction. The basement workshop of the Combine is like nothing so much as the subterranean kitchens of the dreaded Morlocks in H. G. Wells' The Time Machine, and the good lady herself is, of course, one of the ingenious machines that terrorize the Earth in Wells' The War of the Worlds. Finally, the Combine itself, while bearing certain stamps of scientific romance, is actually from the Saturday serials tradition (or more recently the Bond variation) where a shadowy conspiracy threatens the future of mankind. We should not overlook correspondences to the Yellow Peril Menace, overseen by the arch - villain Fu Manchu, either, in light of the anti - "Eastern" perspective of the book. Bromden, too, is an outgrowth in part of popular tradition. He is a Vanishing American (we're led to believe, in fact, that his whole tribe has disintegrated or vanished), certainly, a bearer of the standard of "natural man" against "standardized man." The standard he bears belongs to Tarzan,

Conan, and "The Heap," as well as Tonto, Chingachgook, and Queequeg.

Comics strips, movies and radio shows, then, are clearly seen as setting up terms and conditions for many aspects of *Cuckoo's Nest*. And, of course, one shouldn't forget the snatches of popular song and folk song McMurphy regales the Ward with, each signaling the presence of some important thematic element, interpreting the action, and tying the big redhead to the mystique, eclectically drawn from a variety of forms, of the roving balladeer, the picaro leaving a snatch of song at the site of his conquests.

Our triumvirate of popular - culture heroes and villains operates in a cartoon world, "where the figures are flat and outlined in black, jerking through some kind of goofy story that might be real funny if it weren't for the cartoon figures being real guys." This correspondence that Kesey finds between the world of cartoons and the world of contemporary man is absolutely essential to hold in the forefront of one's mind if one is to truly grasp Kesey's plan in utilizing popular myth to shape his novel. He is telling us, first of all, as clearly as he can that this is no joke, this is real, people and ideas are simple and often simplistic, not recondite, obscure, complex. This is especially true when they have submitted to the conditioning processes of modern life. Kesey understands the popular myths to be ways of understanding what is happening in our world, important interpreters of events. In this he would find powerful support from Marshall McLuhan and especially from his colleague Edmund Carpenter, the Canadian media theorist. Carpenter maintains in a compelling argument that man "becomes what he beholds," - in some sense, then, we can argue that Kesey sees the media regimentation of our lives, even of the formerly chaotic and various popular culture, as the real face of the Combine -

a popular **imagery** supported by "Nest in the West" home developers and the manufacturers of "insect hatch" suits and hats. A world whose horrors and dangers are cast in such terms must be dealt with in similar terms. Or, stated more clearly in reference to *Cuckoo's Nest*, the medicine for a cartoon villain is a cartoon hero-cartoon morality is black and white. Over-intellectualization of the problem leads to a cession of territory to the Bad Guys, a la Dr. Spivey.

We might note, in conclusion, that intensive use of pop - culture imagery stamps *Cuckoo's Nest* as an intensely American product, too, and while this effect is accidental to Kesey's more serious purpose and conscious design, yet it places this work squarely in the mainstream of the major novels of the sixties which work in this native vein.

ONE FLEW OVER THE CUCKOO'S NEST

TOPICS FOR RESEARCH AND CRITICISM

| THEMES

Alienation: R.D. Laing and *Cuckoo's Nest*

Political Control and *Cuckoo's Nest*

Man Creates His Own Gods and Demons

To What Extent Is the Combine "Real"?

Is the Ward a Microcosm of a Larger Reality?

"Anti - Americanism" in *Cuckoo's Nest*

The Individualist and the Group

The Theory of the Therapeutic Community

Man and His Hierarchies

Violence as an Acceptable Strategy for Change

Life as a Gamble vs. Life as a Certainty

Kesey and Woman's Lib

COMPARISON WITH OTHER WORKS

The Literary Debts of *Cuckoo's Nest*

Is Kesey a Black Humorist in the Tradition of Heller, Pynchon, and Vonnegut?

The Existential Vision of Sartre and RPM

RPM and Bromden as Colin Wilson's "Outsider"

Self - Sacrifice in Literature: Sidney Carton to RPM

Cuckoo's Nest as Drama: Changes in the Novel

RPM as Odysseus

Ayn Rand and Randle Patrick McMurphy: A Family Relationship?

KESEY'S OTHER WORK

Cuckoo's Nest and *Sometimes A Great Notion*: Compare and Contrast

Kesey's Fiction: Mirror of His Life?

From *Cuckoo's Nest* to *Garage Sale*: Growth or Degeneration?

The Author's Correspondence

Kesey as Systematic Moralist

The Kesey Cult

The Merry Pranksters as an Art Form

Kesey and the Romantic Tradition

KESEY AS SOCIAL CRITIC

Kesey's Assessment of Woman and Her Traditional Roles

The Medical Profession and *Cuckoo's Nest*

Man and Machine: Identities or Antagonists

The American Indian Experience: Kesey's View

Minority Group Characterizations in *Cuckoo's Nest*

Family Relationships in *Cuckoo's Nest*

The Drug Scene: Implicit Judgments in Kesey's Fiction

Class and Caste in *Cuckoo's Nest*

Kesey's Moral Judgments

"CUCKOO'S NEST" AS A LITERARY WORK

RPM as Christ Figure

Kesey's Prose Style

Function of the Fog Scenes

The Rise and Fall (?) of the Combine

Minor Characters: Conception and Utilization

The Disciple Relationships

RPM's Songs

Function of Games and Gaming in *Cuckoo's Nest*

Bromden and McMurphy: Hero or Anti - Hero?

Character Development in Ratched, McMurphy, and Bromden

Foreshadowing and Reversal in *Cuckoo's Nest*

Ratched as Satan

The Mechanism of Humor in CN: What Turns It On?

Cuckoo's Nest as Parable

Pop Culture **Allusions** in Kesey's Work

BIBLIOGRAPHY

WORKS BY KEN KESEY

One Flew Over the Cuckoo's Nest. New York: Viking, 1962.

Sometimes a Great Notion. New York: Viking, 1964.

Kesey's *Garage Sale.* New York: Viking, 1973 (a collection).

SELECTED WORKS ABOUT KEN KESEY

Barsness, John A. "Ken Kesey: The Hero in Modern Dress." *Bulletin of the Rocky Mountain Modern Language Association,* XXIII, 1 (March 1969), 27–33.

Fiedler, Leslie A. *The Return of the Vanishing American.* New York: Stein and Day, 1968.

_____. "The New Mutants." *Partisan Review,* XXXII, 4 (Fall 1965), 505–29.

Hauck, Richard B. "The Comic Christ and the Modern Reader." *College English,* XXXI, 5 (February 1970), 498–506.

Klein, Marcus, ed. *The American Novel since World War II.* Greenwich, Conn.: Fawcett, 1969.

Malin, Irving. "Ken Kesey: *One Flew Over the Cuckoo's Nest.*" *Critique*, V, 2 (1962), 81–97.

Miller, James E., Jr. *Quests Surd and Absurd.* Chicago: The University of Chicago Press, 1968.

Reich, Charles A. *The Greening of America.* New York: Random House, 1970.

Schopf, William. "Blindfolded and Backwards: Promethean and Bemushroomed Heroism in *One Flew Over the Cuckoo's Nest* and *Catch-22.*" *Bulletin of the Rocky Mountain Modern Language Association*, X, XVI, 3 (Fall 1972), 89–97.

Sherwood, Terry. "*One Flew Over the Cuckoo's Nest* and the Comic Strip." *Critique*, XIII, 1 (1971), 96–109.

Sutherland, Janet. "A Defense of Ken Kesey's *One Flew Over the Cuckoo's Nest,*" *English Journal*, LXI, 1 (January 1972), 28–31.

Tanner, Tony. *City of Words: American Fiction 1950–1970.* New York: Harper & Row, 1971.

Waldmeir, Joseph J. "Only an Occasional Rutabaga: American Fiction since 1945." *Modern Fiction Studies*, XV, 4 (1969–70), 467–81.

_____. "Two Novelists of the Absurd: Heller and Kesey." *Wisconsin Studies in American Literature*, V, 3 (1964), 192–204.

Wolfe, Tom. *The Electric Kool - Aid Acid Test.* New York: Farrar Straus & Giroux, 1968.

Lightning Source UK Ltd.
Milton Keynes UK
UKHW020820121021
392080UK00016B/1068